The
Music
Quotation Book

Sound And Vision

Frontispiece: *The Bookworm*, by Carl Spitzweg (1808-1878)

The Music Lover's Quotation Book

Compiled & Edited by
David W. Barber

Sound And Vision

EDITOR'S NOTE

"After silence," Aldous Huxley says in *Music at Night*, expressing himself rather well, "that which comes nearest to expressing the inexpressible is music."

And that which comes nearest to expressing music, he might have gone on to add — other than the music itself, of course — is people talking or writing about music.

Anthony Burgess, a great writer who was also a musician, often observed (lamented, really) that one of the chief differences between language and music (or between their building blocks, words and notes) is that language generally has to *mean* something. It has to be *about* something. Especially prose — but even poetry, which sometimes tends to be more about sound than sense — generally ends up having to describe or relate to something in the "real" world, even if it's only a fictional one. (He claimed to be not as fond as other people are of his great novel *A Clockwork Orange* because, he said, "the plot kept getting in the way." For him, it was all about the language and the sounds.) Whereas music, Burgess said enviously, gets to be about only itself. (Unless it's program music, like Vivaldi's *The Four Seasons*, or Leroy Anderson's *The Typewriter*, in which case it's more of a musical paint-by-numbers set.)

At any rate, words about music — though maybe not as expressive as performing the music, obviously — are nevertheless often very interesting, and expressive, and evocative and enlightening, in their own right. And so, as Shakespeare says in *Twelfth Night*, "if music be the food of love, play on ..."

DWB,
Toronto, 2003

ABILITY

We all have ability. The difference is how we use it.
> – Stevie (b. Steveland Judkins) Wonder (b.1950),
> American singer-songwriter, pianist

We are all more capable than we think we are.
> – Anne Murray (b.1945),
> Canadian popular singer, performer

ABSTRACT MUSIC

There is no such thing as Abstract Music; there is good music and bad music. If it is good, it means something — and then it is Program Music.
> – Richard Strauss (1864-1949),
> German composer

Nothing is more odious than music without hidden meaning.
> – Frédéric Chopin (1810-49),
> Polish-born French composer,
> in *La Courrier musical* (1910)

I cannot conceive of music that expresses absolutely nothing.
– Bela Bartok (1881-1945),
Hungarian composer

ACCOMPANIST

No singer is a hero to his own accompanist.

– Anon.

ACCORDION

I am not a demon. I am a lizard, a shark, a heat-seeking panther. I want to be Bob Denver on acid playing the accordion.
– Nicolas Cage (b.1964),
American film actor

A gentleman is a man who can play the accordion but doesn't.
– Anon.

Accordion, n. An instrument with the sentiments of an assassin.
– Ambrose Bierce (1842-1914),
American journalist, writer,
in *The Devil's Dictionary* (1906)

ADVICE

When a piece gets difficult, make faces.
– Artur Schnabel (1882-1951),
Austrian pianist, composer,
giving advice to fellow pianist Vladimir Horowitz

Nature has given us two ears but only one mouth.
– Benjamin Disraeli (1804-81),
English Prime Minister

In case of emergency:
    1. Grab your coat.
    2. Take your hat.
    3. Leave your worries on the doorstep.
    4. Direct your feet to the sunny side of the street.

– Anon.

To be played with both hands in the pocket.

– Erik Satie (1866-1925),
French composer,
instructions for one of his piano pieces

Consort not with a female musician lest thou be taken in by her snares.

– Ben Sira,
The Book of Wisdom (ca. 190 BC)

The high note is not the only thing.

– Placido Domingo (b.1941),
Spanish opera singer

Don't do unto others as you would have them do unto you — their tastes may be different.

– George Bernard Shaw (1856-1950),
Irish-English playwright, music critic, wit

I would advise you to keep your overhead down; avoid a major drug habit; play every day; and take it in front of other people. They need to hear it, and you need them to hear it.

– James Taylor (b.1948),
American singer-songwriter

Life is 10% what you make it, and 90% how you take it.

– Irving (Israel Baline) Berlin (1888-1989),
Russian-American composer, pianist

Act the way you'd like to be and soon you'll be the way you act.

– Leonard Cohen (b.1934),
Canadian poet, singer-songwriter

Just don't give up trying to do what you really want to do. Where there is love and inspiration, I don't think you can go wrong.

> – Ella Fitzgerald (1918-96),
> American jazz singer

AGE

O! sir, I must not tell my age. They say women and music should never be dated.

> – Oliver Goldsmith (1728-74),
> Irish playwright,
> Miss Hardcastle in *She Stoops to Conquer* (1773)

It's all right letting yourself go, as long as you can get yourself back.

> – Mick Jagger (b.1943)
> English singer-songwriter, performer
> (The Rolling Stones)

AGENT(S)

An agent is a person who is sore because an actor gets 90% of what they make.

> – Sir Elton (Reginald Kenneth Dwight) John (b.1947),
> English singer-songwriter,
> composer, pianist

ALCOHOL

I don't drink because I'm an alcoholic. I drink because I love to party.

> – Bret (Sychak) Michaels
> (b.1962),
> American singer-songwriter
> (Poison)

You think I'm an asshole now, you should have seen me when
I was drunk.
– John Mellencamp (b.1951),
American singer-songwriter

AMATEURS

Hell is full of musical amateurs. Music is the brandy of the
damned.
– George Bernard Shaw (1856-1950),
Irish-English playwright, music critic, wit
in *Man and Superman* (1903)

The Artistic Temperament is a disease that afflicts amateurs.
– G.K. Chesterton (1874-1936),
English writer, critic

Said Oscar Wilde: 'Each man kills the thing he loves.' For
example, the amateur musician.
– H.L. Mencken (1880-1956),
American journalist, writer, music critic

AMERICA

I had always loved beautiful and artistic things, though before
leaving America I had had a very little chance of seeing any.
– Emma Albani
(born Marie Louise Emma Cecile Lajeunesse, 1847-1930),
Canadian opera and concert singer

AMERICAN MUSIC

The way to write American music is simple. All you have to do
is be an American and then write any kind of music you wish.
– Virgil Thompson (1896-1989),
American composer, music critic

ANGUISH

I hear a gay modulating anguish, rather like music.
— Christopher Fry (b.1907),
English playwright,
The Lady's Not for Burning (1949)

APPLAUSE

Applause is a receipt, not a note of demand.
— Artur Schnabel (1882-1951),
Austrian pianist, composer

ARCHITECTURE

Writing about art is like dancing about architecture.
— Anon. (variously attributed)

Music, theoretically considered, consists altogether of lines of tone. It more nearly resembles a picture or an architectural drawing, than any other art creation; the difference being that in a drawing the lines are visible and constant, while in music they are audible and in motion. The separate tones are the points through which the lines are drawn; and the impression which is intended, and which is apprehended by the intelligent listener, is not that of single tones, but of continuous lines of tones, describing movements, curves and angles, rising, falling, poising – directly analogous to the linear impressions conveyed by a picture or drawing.
— Percy Goetschius (1853–1943),
American music critic, theorist,
Elementary Counterpoint

I call architecture frozen music.
— Johann Wolfgang von Goethe (1749-1832),
German writer, philosopher,
in a letter to Johann Peter Eckermann (March 1829)

Since [architecture] is music in space, as it were a frozen music.

> – Friedrich von Schelling (1715-1854),
> German philosopher, writer,
> *Philosophie der Kunst* (*Philosophy of Art,* 1809)

Architecture, said Hegel, is frozen music, as you'll remember; Donald Swann's music is often being compared with defrosted architecture.

> – Michael Flanders (1922-75),
> English singer, lyricist, comedic pianist,
> *At the Drop of a Hat*

ARMSTRONG, LOUIS

How did I feel when I first got the call that I was booked for *Sports Illustrated*? How did Louis Armstrong feel when he first walked on the moon?

> Rebecca Romijn-Stamos (b.1972),
> American supermodel, actress

ARMY

I figured I'd better do it while there was a hiatus between wars.

> – Tom Lehrer (b.1928),
> American singer-songwriter, mathematician,
> on why (in 1955) he joined the U.S. Army

ART

The trouble, Mr. Goldwyn, is that you are only interested in art and I am only interested in money.

> – George Bernard Shaw (1856-1950),
> Irish-English playwright, music critic, wit
> to Sam Goldwyn (1882-1974), American movie producer,
> who wanted Shaw to write for Hollywood movies

Art distils sensation and embodies it with meaning in
memorable form — or else it is not art.

> – Jacques Barzun (b.1907),
> French-American writer, historian,
> *The House of Intellect* (1959)

Art is a revolt against fate.

> – André Malraux (1901-76),
> French writer, statesman

Art is born of humiliation.

> – W. H. Auden (1907-73),
> English poet

Art is a collaboration between God and the artist, and the
less the artist does the better.

> – André Gide (1869-1951),
> French novelist, writer

All art constantly aspires towards the condition of music.

> – Walter Pater (1839-94),
> English essayist, critic,
> *The Renaissance: The School of Giorgione* (1873)

All the arts in America are a gigantic racket run by unscrupulous men for unhealthy women.
— Sir Thomas Beecham (1879-1961),
English conductor, in the London *Observer* (May 1946)

It is enough to get on with the task of creating art without asking why one is doing it.
— Anthony Burgess (1917-93),
English novelist, composer,
This Man and Music (1983)

ARTIST

An artist is his own fault.
— John O'Hara (1905-70),
American writer

ATTITUDES

Our attitudes control our lives. Attitudes are a secret power working 24 hours a day, for good or bad. It is of paramount importance that we know how to harness and control this great force.
— Irving (Israel Baline) Berlin (1888-1989),
Russian-American composer, pianist

AUDIENCE PARTICIPATION

Will people in the cheaper seats clap your hands? All the rest of you, if you'll just rattle your jewelry ...
— John Lennon (1940-80),
English musician singer-songwriter, (The Beatles),
at a Royal command performance (1963)

If you feel like singing along, don't.
— James Taylor (b.1948),
American singer-songwriter, to an audience

Together we should sing it,
It's just a children's song.
And if you do not know the words,
— You'd better learn them!
> — Peter, Paul and Mary,
> American folk trio,
> in a concert version of *Puff, The Magic Dragon.*

AUDIENCE(S)

Hell is a half-filled auditorium.
> — Robert Frost (1874-1963),
> American poet

I know two kinds of audience only — one coughing and one not coughing.
> — Artur Schnabel (1882-1951),
> Austrian pianist, composer,
> in *My Life and Music* (1961)

That reminds me, I'm playing a concert tonight.
> — Fritz Kreisler (1875-1962),
> Austrian violinist,
> on seeing a row of fish at the market

[Wilhelm] Furtwängler, was once told in Berlin that the people in the back seats were complaining that they could not hear some of his soft passages. "It does not matter," he said, "they do not pay so much."
> — Neville Cardus (1889-1975),
> English music critic, writer,
> in *The Manchester Guardian* (1935)

Flint must be an extremely wealthy town: I see that each of you bought two or three seats.
> — Victor Borge (1909-2000),
> Danish-American musical humorist, pianist,
> speaking to a half-full house in Flint, Michigan

Not content to have the audience in the palm of his hand, he goes one further and clenches his fist.
— Kenneth Tynan (1927-80),
English journalist, writer, critic,
on American singer Frankie Laine
(born Frank Paul LoVecchio, 1913)

The audience strummed their cattarhs.
— Alexander Woollcott (1887-1943),
American journalist, critic

AUDITIONS

It was the kind of show where the girls were are not auditioned — just measured.
— Irene Thomas (b.1920)
English writer, broadcaster

AUTHORITY

I don't like authority, at least I don't like other people's authority.
— A.C. Benson (1862-1925),
English writer, hymn lyricist (*Land of Hope and Glory*,
set to music by Sir Edward Elgar), in *Letters to M.E.A.* (1926)

BACH, J.S.

Whether the angels play only Bach in praising God I am not quite sure; I am sure, however, that *en famille* they play Mozart.

> – Karl Barth (1886-1968),
> Swiss theologian, writer,
> quoted in *The New York Times* (Dec. 1968)

The miracle of Bach has not appeared in any other art. To strip human nature until its divine attributes are made clear, to inform ordinary activities with spiritual fervor, to give wings of eternity to that which is most ephemeral; to make divine things human and human things divine; such is Bach, the greatest and purest moment in music of all time.

> – Pablo Casals (1876-1973),
> Spanish cellist, writer
> in *Conversations With Casals*, ed. J.M. Corredor (1956)

Bach and myself write with the individual performer in mind.

> – "Duke" (Edward Kennedy) Ellington (1889-1974),
> American jazz pianist, composer, bandleader (1977)

You want something by Bach? Which one, Johann Sebastian or Jacques Offen?

> – Victor Borge (1909-2000),
> Danish-American musical humorist, pianist

There's no reason we can't be friends. We both play Bach. You in your way, I in his.

> – Wanda Landowska (1879-1959),
> Polish concert pianist, to a rival (often named as
> American pianist Rosalyn Turek,(b.1914). (attrib.)

Even Bach comes down to the basic suck, blow, suck, suck, blow.

> – Larry Adler (1914-2001),
> American harmonica virtuoso, writer

BAD MUSIC

Dear Mr. Edison: For myself, I can only say that I am astonished and somewhat terrified at the result of this evening's experiment. Astonished at the wonderful form you have developed and terrified at the thought that so much hideous and bad music will be put on records forever.

> – Sir Arthur Sullivan (1842-1900),
> English composer, on a "phonogram"
> to American inventor Thomas Edison (1888)

If one plays good music, people don't listen, and if one plays bad music, people don't talk.

> – Oscar Wilde (1854-1900),
> Irish-English playwright, novelist, wit,
> *The Importance of Being Earnest* (1895)

If one hears bad music, it is one's duty to drown it by one's conversation.

> – Oscar Wilde (1854-1900),
> Irish-English playwright, novelist, wit
> in *The Picture of Dorian Gray* (1891)

Extraordinary how potent cheap music is!

> – Sir Noel Coward (1899-1973),
> English playwright, singer-songwriter, actor, wit

There is a lot of bad music in every age, and there is no reason why this one should be an exception.

> – Harold C. Schonberg (b.1915),
> American writer, historian
> *New York Times* music critic (March 1961)

BAGPIPES

The Irish gave the bagpipes to the Scots as a joke, but the Scots haven't seen the joke yet.

> – Oliver Herford (1863-1935),
> American author, artist

Others, when the bag-pipe sings i' the nose,
Cannot contain their urine.
— William Shakespeare, (1564-1616),
English poet, playwright,
Shylock, in *The Merchant of Venice*,
act 4, scene 1. lines 49-50

BALLET

I don't understand anything
about the ballet. All I know is
that during the intervals the
ballerinas stink like horses.
— Anton Chekov (1860-1904),
Russian playwright, poet

BANJO

I can see fiddling around with
a banjo, but how do you banjo
around with a fiddle?
— Duncan Purney,
in *Musical Notes* (May 1984)

BAROQUE MUSIC

Muzak for the intelligensia.
— Anon. on Baroque music, circa 1970

BARTOK, BELA

He not only never wears his heart on his sleeve; he seems to
have deposited it in some bank vault.
— Colin Wilson (b.1931),
English writer, philosopher,
on Hungarian composer Bela Bartok (1881-1945),
in *Brandy of the Damned* (1964)

BEATLES

John Lennon, Paul McCartney and George Harrison are the greatest composers since Beethoven, with Paul McCartney way out in front.

– Richard Buckle (b.1916),
English journalist,
in the *Sunday Times* (Dec. 1963)

BEAUTY

The Beautiful arises from the perceived harmony of an object, whether sight or sound.

– Samuel Taylor Coleridge (1772-1834),
English poet, writer,
On the Principals of Genial Criticism (1814)

BED

'Bed,' as the Italian proverb succinctly puts it, 'is the poor man's opera.'

– Aldous Huxley (1894-1963),
English writer, essayist,
Heaven and Hell (1956)

BEDPOST

Does the Spearmint Lose Its Flavor on the Bedpost Overnight?
– Billy Rose (1899-1966)
and Marty Bloom (Martin L. Blumenthal), song title (1924),
music by Ernest Breuer. Revived by Lonnie Donegan as
Does Your Chewing Gum Lose Its Flavor... (1959)

BEECHAM, SIR THOMAS

Hark! the herald angels sing!
Beecham's Pills are just the thing,
Two for a woman, one for a child,
Peace on earth and mercy mild!
> – Sir Thomas Beecham (1879-1961),
> English conductor

At a rehearsal I let the orchestra play as they like. At the concert I make them play as *I* like.
> – Sir Thomas Beecham (1879-1961),
> English conductor

BEETHOVEN, LUDWIG VAN

If Beethoven had been killed in a plane crash at the age of 22, it would have changed the history of music – and of aviation.
> – Tom Stoppard (b.1937),
> Czech-English playwright, writer, wit

I occasionally play works by contemporary composers for two reasons. First to discourage the composer from writing any more and secondly to remind myself how much I appreciate Beethoven.
> – Jascha Heifetz (1901-87),
> Russian-American violinist

It is impossible to imagine Goethe or Beethoven being good at billiards or golf.
> – H.L. Mencken (1880-1956),
> American journalist, writer,
> music critic

Last night the band played Beethoven. Beethoven lost.
– Anon.

Beethoven always sounds to me like the upsetting of a bag
of nails, with here and there an also dropped hammer.
– John Ruskin (1819-1900),
English art critic, writer, essayist,
in a letter to John Brown (Feb, 1881)

I love Beethoven, especially the poems.
– Ringo (Richard Starkey) Starr (b.1940),
English musician, singer-songwriter (The Beatles)

You can chase a Beethoven symphony all your life and never
catch up.
– André Previn (b.1929),
French-American conductor

BELLS

Ride a cockhorse to Banbury Cross,
To see a fine lady upon a white horse;
Rings on her fingers and bells on her toes,
She shall have music wherever she goes.
– *Ride a Cockhorse*,
English nursery rhyme from the 15th century

BERG, ALBAN

It is my private opinion that [Alban] Berg is just a bluff. But
even if he isn't, it is impossible to deny that his music (?) is a
soporiphic, by the side of which the telephone book is a strong
cup of coffee.
– Samuel Chotzinoff,
in the *New York Post* (April 1935)

BERLIOZ, HECTOR

Berlioz says nothing in his music, but he says it magnifcently.
> – James Gibbons Huncker (1860-1921),
> American music critic, writer

BIOGRAPHY

My name is Hugo Wolf. I was born on March 13th 1860, and am still alive at the moment. That's biography enough.
> – Hugo Wolf (1860-1903),
> Austrian composer, writer,
> replying to a request for biographical information

BIRD(S)

I played more or less as a bird sings, instinctively, uncalculatingly, unthinkingly.
> – Sir Yehudi Menuhin (1916-1999),
> American-English, violinist, conductor, writer,
> in *Menuhin* (1976)

There is a singer everyone has heard,
Loud, a mid-summer and a mid-wood bird,
Who makes the solid tree trunks sound again.
...
The bird would cease and be as other birds
But that he knows in singing not to sing.
The question that he frames in all but words
Is what to make of a diminished thing.
> – Robert Frost (1874-1963),
> American poet, writer,
> *The Oven Bird* (*Mountain Interval,* 1916)

The time to hear bird music is between four and six in the morning. Seven o'clock is not too late, but by eight the fine rapture is over, due, I suspect, to the contentment of the inner man that comes with breakfast; a poet should always be hungry or have a lost love.
> – Donald Culross Peattie (1898-1964),
> American botanist, poet,
> in *An Almanac for Moderns* (1935)

He would declare and could himself believe
That the birds there in all the garden round
From having heard the daylong voice of Eve
Had added to their own an oversound,
Her tone of meaning but without the words.
Admittedly an eloquence so soft
Could only have had an influence on birds
When call or laughter carried it aloft.
Be that as it may, she was in their song.
Moreover her voice upon their voices crossed
Had now persisted in the woods so long
That probably it never would be lost.
Never again would birds' song be the same.
And to do that to birds was why she came.
> – Robert Frost (1874-1963),
> American poet, writer
> *Never Again Would Birds' Song Be the Same*
> (*A Witness Tree*, 1942)

Sweet bird, that shunn'st the noise of folly,
Most musical, most melancholy!
> – John Milton (1608-74),
> English poet,
> *Il Penseroso* (1632)

BLASPHEMY

All great truths begin as blasphemies.
> – George Bernard Shaw (1856-1950),
> Irish-English playwright, music critic, wit,
> *Annajanska* (1919)

B-minor Mass

Why waste money on psychotherapy when you can listen to the *B-minor Mass?*

> Michael Torke (b.1961),
> American composer,
> on J.S. Bach's masterpiece

Blues

I've said that playing the blues is like having to be black twice. Stevie [Ray Vaughan] missed on both counts, but I never noticed.

> – B. B. (Riley) King (b.1925),
> American blues guitarist, singer-songwriter

Book

The possession of a book becomes a substitute for reading it.

> – Anthony Burgess (1917-93),
> English novelist, composer,
> in the *New York Times Book Review* (Dec. 1966)

Bowels

Wherefore shall my bowels sound as an harp for Moab.

> – *Isaiah* 16:11

Brahms, Johannes

Art is long and life is short: here is evidently the explanation of a Brahms symphony.

> – Edward Lorne,
> in *Fanfare*, London (Jan. 1922)

I played over the music of that scoundrel Brahms. What a giftless bastard! It annoys me that this self-inflated mediocrity is hailed as a genius.
– Peter Ilych Tchaikovsky (1840-93)
Russian composer on Johannes Brahms (1833-97),
diary entry, Oct, 1886 in *Lexicon of Musical Invective*,
ed. Nicolas Slonimsky

[Brahms is] rather tiresomely addicted to dressing himself up as Handel or Beethoven and making a prolonged and intolerable noise.
– George Bernard Shaw (1856-1950),
Irish-English playwright, music critic, wit
in *The World* (June 1893)

If there is anyone here whom I have not insulted, I beg his pardon.
– Johannes Brahms (1833-97),
German composer,
on leaving a party of friends (attrib.)

BRAHMS *REQUIEM*

The Brahms *Requiem* is patiently borne only by the corpse.
– George Bernard Shaw (1856-1950),
Irish-English playwright, music critic, wit

There are some experiences in life which should not be demanded twice from any man, and one of them is listening to the Brahms *Requiem*.
– George Bernard Shaw (1856-1950),
Irish-English playwright, music critic, wit

Brahms's *Requiem* has not the true funeral relish: It is so execrably and ponderously dull that the very flattest of funerals would seem like a ballet, or at least a *danse macabre*, after it.
– George Bernard Shaw (1856-1950),
Irish-English playwright, music critic, wit,
in *The World* (November 1892)

BRASS

Brass bands are all very well in their place – outdoors and
several miles away.

> – Sir Thomas Beecham (1879-1961),
> English conductor (attrib.)

Never look encouragingly at the brass, except with a short
glance to give them an important cue. But never let the horns
and woodwind out of your sight: if you can hear them at all they
are still too strong.

> – Richard Strauss (1864-1949),
> German composer,
> advice to a conductor, circa 1922, published
> in *Betrachtungen und Erinnerungen*
> (*Recollections and Reflections*, 1949)

BREAD

Music I heard with you was more
than music,
And bread I broke with you
was more than bread.
Now that I am without you,
all is desolate;
All that was once so beautiful
is dead.

> – Conrad Aiken (1889–1973),
> American poet, writer *Discordants:*
> *Bread and Music* (1914)

BUSH, GEORGE W.

Just so you know, we're ashamed the
president of the United States is from Texas.

> – Natalie Maines (b.1974),
> American country singer-songwriter (Dixie Chicks),
> before the Iraq War (March 2003)

I feel the president is ignoring the opinions of many in the U.S. and alienating the rest of the world. My comments were made in frustration, and one of the privileges of being an American is you are free to voice your own point of view.
– Natalie Maines (b.1974),
American country singer-songwriter (Dixie Chicks),
apologizing for her earlier remark (March 2003)

He's not necessarily stupid, he's just obviously done a little too much cocaine.
– Ashley MacIsaac (b.1974),
Canadian musician, fiddler,
quoted in the *National Post* (April 2003)

CANON

Canon: ... Not to be confused with the ones required in the *1812 Overture*, which are spelt differently and which lack contrapuntal interest.
– Anthony Hopkins,
in *Downbeat Music Guide* (1977)

CAREER

There wasn't really a career to speak of. I figure I wrote 37 songs in 20 years, and that's not exactly a full-time job.
– Tom Lehrer (b.1928),
American singer-songwriter, mathematician,
on giving up his songwriting career,
in an interview with *The Onion*

It's just a cool thing to do and my decisions for my career have nothing to do with my personal life.
– Justin Timberlake (b.1981),
American singer-songwriter, performer,
on sharing the stage with Christina Aguilera, pop rival to
Timberlake's ex-girlfriend Britney Spears,
quoted in *Inside Entertainment* (Summer 2003)

CARES

Music for a while shall all your cares beguile
                              – Anon., for the masque *Oedipus* (1692?),
                              set to music by Henry Purcell (1659-95)

CELLO

The cello is not one of my favorite instruments. It has such a lugubrious sounds, like someone reading a will.
                              – Irene Thomas (b.1920),
                              English writer, broadcaster

Madame, there you sit with that magnificent instrument between your legs, and all you can do is *scratch* it!
                              – Arturo Toscanini (1867-1957),
                              Italian conductor, to a woman cellist.
                    Also often attrib. to Sir Thomas Beecham (*q.v.*)

CEREMONY

Those who seek to satisfy the mind of man by hampering it with ceremonies and music and affecting charity and devotion have lost their original nature.
                              – Chuang Tzu (369-286 B.C),
                    Chinese philosopher, writer, poet, *Joined Toes*

CHARM(S)

Music has charms to soothe a savage breast,
To soften rocks, or bend a knotted oak.
                              – William Congreve (1670–1729),
                              English dramatist, writer
                    Almeria, in *The Mourning Bride* (1697)
                    (Often misquoted as "hath" and "savage beast")

Music oft hath such a charm
To make bad good, and good provoke to harm.
> – William Shakespeare (1564-1616),
> English poet, playwright,
> Duke Vincentio, in *Measure for Measure*,
> act 4, scene 1, line 16

Music hath charms to soothe the savage beast, but I'd try a revolver first.
> – Josh Billings (1818-85),
> American humorist, writer

CHURCH

As some to church repair,
Not for the doctrine, but the music there.
> – Alexander Pope (1688-1744),
> English poet,
> *An Essay on Criticism* (1711)

COMEDY

Comedy is very important, yes. For one thing, it keeps you sane.
> – Tom Lehrer (b.1928),
> American singer-songwriter, mathematician,
> in an interview with *The Onion*

COMMERCIALS

My favorite music is the sound of radio commercials at 10 dollars a whack.
> – Lord Roy Thomson of Fleet (1894-1976),
> Canadian-English newspaper press baron

CLASSICAL MUSIC

Classical music is music written by famous dead foreigners.
— Arlene Heath

Classical music is the kind we keep thinking will turn into a tune.
— "Kin" Frank Hubbard McKinny (1868-1930),
American newspaer editor, journalist, writer, wit,
Comments of Abe Martin and His Neighbors (1923)

COMPOSERS AND COMPOSING

You have to develop in many different directions, because composers are so useless.
— John Beckwith (b.1927),
Canadian critic, essayist, educator, composer,
quoted in *The Globe and Mail* (Jan. 1998)

Give me a laundry list and I'll set it to music.
— Gioacchino Rossini (1792-1868),
Italian composer

Before I compose a piece, I walk round it several times, accompanied by myself.
— Erik Satie (1866-1925),
French composer (1913)

The main thing the public demands of a composer is that he be dead.
— Arthur Honneger (1892-1955),
French composer, (when he was still alive)

Composition is notation of distortion of what composers think they've heard before. Masterpieces are marvelous misquotations.
— Ned Rorem (b.1923),
American composer, writer,
The Paris Diary of Ned Rorem (1966)

If a composer could state in words what being a composer means, he would no longer need to be a composer.
– Ned Rorem (b.1923),
American composer, writer,
Critical Affairs (1970)

Good music resembles something. It resembles the composer.
– Jean Cocteau (1889-1963),
French film director, dramatist, writer, poet
Cock and Harlequin (1918)

Composing is like making love to the future.
– Lukas Foss (b.1922),
American composer, pianist, conductor,

Music is now so foolish that I am amazed. Everything that is wrong is permitted, and no attention is paid to what the old generation wrote as composition.
– Samuel Scheidt (1587-1654),
German composer

The good composer is slowly discovered; the bad composer is slowly found out.
– Ernest Newman (1868-1959),
English music critic, writer

Composers shouldn't think too much — it interferes with their plagiarism.
– Howard Dietz (1896-1983),
American lyricist, composer

When I was young, people used to say to me: Wait until you're 50, you'll see. I am 50. I haven't seen anything.
– Erik Satie (1866-1925),
French composer (1913)

In order to compose, all you need to do is remember a tune that nobody else has thought of.
– Robert Schumann (1810-56),
German composer

Never compose anything unless not composing it becomes a positive nuisance to you.

> – Gustav Holst (1874-1934),
> English composer

COMPULSION

Such sweet compulsion doth in music lie.

> – John Milton (1608-74),
> English poet,
> *Arcades* (1630-34)

CONDUCTORS AND CONDUCTING

I kissed my first girl and smoked my first cigarette on the same day. I haven't had time for tobacco since.

> – Arturo Toscanini (1867-1957),
> Italian conductor

There's only one woman I know of who could never be a symphony conductor, and that's the Venus de Milo.

> – Margaret Hillis (b.1921),
> American conductor, writer

I've been a woman for a little over 50 years and have gotten over my initial astonishment. As for conducting an orchestra, that's a job where I don't think sex plays much part.

> – Nadia Boulanger (1887-1979),
> French composer, conductor, teacher

There are two golden rules for an orchestra: start together and finish together. The public doesn't give a damn what goes on in between.

> – Sir Thomas Beecham (1879-1961),
> English conductor

This backward man, this view obstructor,
Is known to us as the conductor.

> – Lawrence McKinney

I am not the greatest conductor in this country. On the other hand, I'm better than any damned foreigner.

> – Sir Thomas Beecham (1879-1961),
> English conductor,
> in the *Daily Express* (Mar. 1961)

Why do we have to have all these third-rate foreign conductors around – when we have so many second-rate ones of our own?

> – Sir Thomas Beecham(1879-1961),
> English conductor

They are for prima donnas or corpses — I am neither.

> – Arturo Toscanini (1867-1957),
> Italian conductor,
> refusing a wreath of flowers after a concert

After I die, I shall return to Earth as a gatekeeper of a bordello and I won't let any of you — not a one of you — enter!

> – Arturo Toscanini (1867-1957),
> Italian conductor,
> to an orchestra during rehearsal

Can't you read? The score demands *con amore*, and what are you doing? You are playing it like married men!

> – Arturo Toscanini (1867-1957),
> Italian conductor,
> to an orchestra during rehearsal

We cannot expect you to be with us all the time, but perhaps you could be good enough to keep in touch now and again.

> – Sir Thomas Beecham (1879-1961),
> English conductor,
> to a soloist during rehearsal

COUNTRY MUSIC

Country music is three chords and the truth.
> – Harlan Howard (1927-2002),
> American country singer-songwriter

Country music is still your grandpa's music, but it's also your daughter's music. It's getting bigger and better all the time and I'm glad to be a part of it.
> – Shania Twain (b.1965),
> Canadian country singer-songwriter, performer

There's a lot of things blamed on me that never happened. But then, there's a lot of things that I did that I never got caught at.
> – Johnny Cash (b.1932),
> American country singer-songwriter

COWARD, SIR NOEL

Forty years ago [Noel Coward] was Slightly in *Peter Pan*, and you might say that he has been wholly in *Peter Pan* ever since.
> – Kenneth Tynan (1927-80),
> English journalist, writer, critic,
> in *Curtains* (1961)

CREATIVITY

All men are creative but few are artists.
> – Paul Goodman (1911-72),
> American poet, writer,
> in *Growing Up Absurd* (1961)

It seems to me that those songs that have been any good, I have nothing much to do with the writing of them. The words have just crawled down my sleeve and come out on the page.
> – Joan Baez (b.1941),
> American singer-songwriter, activist

Sometimes, you can write some pretty mad stuff when you're off your head. And then, the next day, when you come back down to Earth, with the horror of the most hideous of bumps, in full toxic shock, you look back at what you've written and you either just chuck it away in disgust or you add a bit to it with the proper hangover, the proper comedown.

You end up with loads of Post-it Notes and stickies, and bits torn out of magazines with words on them, and you put them together.

Whether you're still off your head or whether you've got a hangover, you're in this human state where it's all about just existing. You're not worried. You haven't got time to think about all the crap that's normally going on in your head. When you do a vocal, for instance, you're not sitting there thinking about bills or shit at home or repairs to the bathroom or what new American walk-in fridge you want to buy. You're straight in there with the song and you've got in your head and the fear you've got in your heart. It is quite a scary, precarious place.

> – Robert "3D" Del Naja (b.1967),
> English pop vocalist (Massive Attack),
> quoted in the *National Post* (Feb. 2003)

Creativity is more than just being different. Anybody can play weird; that's easy. What's hard is to be as simple as Bach. Making the simple, awesomely simple, that's creativity.

> – Charles Mingus (b.1922),
> American jazz musician, composer

That's when the creativity starts to dry up, when you take yourself too seriously. You're not natural, and you're not free. When it's just natural and joyous, it turns you on properly.

> – Robert "3D" Del Naja (b.1967),
> English musician, singer-songwriter
> (Massive Attack), quoted in the *National Post* (Feb, 2003)

When you're totally engrossed in a piece of music, it may be taking you somewhere that a lot of people ain't going, purely because it's been so personal to you. When it finally gets to that finished piece, it's quite mind blowing to come back down and then just go and make yourself a cup of tea or take a shit or go across the road and get a paper. You've just spent five hours in the studio going out of your mind. It's the balance thing. ...

I think when you sign on to anything in life truly – whether it be a writer or a musician or any job – you kind of do go to a crossroads situation where you either take it seriously and take it to the extreme or you don't. I did that a few years ago. That entails melodies haunting you, not being able to sleep properly – you know what I mean? It's like you see an athlete at the top, they have to sacrifice something, and I think a musician has to sacrifice quite a big chunk of his mind.

> – "Mad Richard" Ashcroft (b.1971),
> English musician, singer-songwriter, (The Verve),
> quoted in the *National Post* (March 2003)

CREDO

The *Credo* is the longest movment. There is much to believe.

> – Igor Stravinsky (1882-1971),
> Russian-American composer,
> commenting on his *Mass*

CRITICS AND CRITICISM

A statue has never been set up in honor of a critic.

> – Jean Sibelius (1865-1957),
> Finnish composer

A critic is a man who knows the way but can't drive the car.
— Kenneth Tynan (1927-1980),
English journalist, writer, critic

Critics are like eunuchs in a harem. They're there every night, they see it done every night, they see how it should be done every night, but they can't do it themselves.
— Brendan Behan (1923-64),
Irish-American playwright, poet, writer

A critic is a legless man who teaches running.
— Channing Pollock (1880-1946),
American writer, lyricist

I don't base my career on middle-aged pundits.
— Ashley MacIsaac (b.1974),
Canadian musician, fiddler
quoted in the *National Post* (April 2003)

I am sitting in the smallest room of my house. I have your review before me. In a moment it will be behind me.
— Max Reger (1873-1916),
German composer, educator, writer,
responding to critic Rudolf Louis (1906)

I cried all the way to the bank.
— Liberace (Vladzin Valentino) Liberace, 1919-87),
American pianist, performer,
on his reaction to criticism

You know, the critics never change; I'm still getting the same notices I used to get as a child. They tell me I play very well for my age.
— Mischa (Mikail) Elman (1891-1967),
Ukrainian violinist, in his 70s

Critics can't even make music by rubbing their back legs together.
— Mel Brooks (b.1927),
American film director, writer, actor,
in *The New York Times* (1975)

Nature fits all her children with something to do,
He would write and can't write can surely review.
> – James Russell Lowell (1819-91),
> American poet, critic, editor,
> *A Fable for Critics* (1848)

I had another dream the other day about music critics. They were small and rodent-like with padlocked ears, as if they had stepped out of a painting by Goya.
> – Igor Stravinsky (1882-1971),
> Russian-American composer,
> in *The Evening Standard* (Oct. 1969)

The trouble with music critics is that so often they have the score in their hands and not in their heads.
> – Sir Thomas Beecham (1879-1961),
> English conductor

A critic is a necessary evil, and criticism is an evil necessity.
> – Carolyn Wells (1869-1942),
> American writer

[The critic] is forced to be literate about the illiterate, witty about the witless and coherent about the incoherent.
> – John Crosby,
> English music critic, writer

Critics don't buy records. They get 'em free.
> – Nat "King" (Nathaniel Adams Coles) Cole, 1919-65),
> American jazz singer-songwriter, pianist

The lot of critics is to be remembered for what they failed to understand.
> – George Moore
> American writer, critic

Never speak ill of yourself; your friends will always say enough on that subject.
> – Charles M. de Talleyrand-Périgord (1754-1838),
> French diplomat, writer

Last year, I gave several lectures on 'Intelligence and Musicality in Animals.' Today, I shall speak to you about 'Intelligence and Musicality in Critics.' The subject is very similar.

> – Erik Satie (1866-1925),
> French composer,
> in a lecture *In Praise of Critics* (1918)

Criticism of our contemporaries is not criticism; it is conversation.

> – Jules Lamaître

If critics have problems with my personal life, it's their problem. Anybody with half a brain would realize that it's the charts that count.

> – Mariah Carey (b.1971),
> American singer, performer

The music of *The Love for Three Oranges*, I fear, is too much for this generation. After intensive study and close observation at rehearsal and performance, I detected the beginnings of two tunes.

> – Edward Moore,(1873-1958)
> English writer, critic
> Chicago *Tribune* (Dec. 1921)

I found myself referring to the programme to find out whether I ought to be seeing red or looking blue at certain moments, and some of it made many of the audience feel green.

> – The London *Times* (1922),
> reviewing *A Colour Symphony*,
> by English composer Sir Arthur Bliss (1891-1975)

A critic is a bunch of biases held loosely together by a sense of taste.

> – Witney Balliett,
> American music writer for *The New Yorker,*
> *Dinosaurs in the Morning* (1962)

When Frank Sinatra, Jr. was kidnapped, I said "It must have been done by music critics."
— Oscar Levant (1906-72),
American pianist, actor,
in *Memoirs of an Amnesiac* (1965)

I paid a shilling for my programme. The editor informs me with the law of libel in its present unsatisfactory condition, I must not call this a fraud, a cheat, a swindle, an imposition, an exorbitance, or even an overcharge.
— George Bernard Shaw (1856-1950),
Irish-English playwright, music critic, wit

Honest criticism is hard to take, particularly from a relative, a friend, an acquaintance or a stranger.
— Franklin P. Jones

It sounds as if someone had smeared the score of *Tristan* while it was still wet.
— Unnamed contemporary,
on Arnold Schoenberg's *Verklärte Nacht*

Pornophony
— Unnamed American critic,
on *Lady Macbeth of Mtensk*,
opera by Russian composer Dimitri Shostakovich (1906-75)

I can take any amount of criticism, so long as it is unqualified praise.
— Sir Noel Coward (1899-1973),
English playwright, singer-songwriter, actor, wit

The audience came out whistling the set.
— Anonymous critic,
on Irving Berlin's *Miss Liberty* (1949)

Assassination is the extreme form of censorship.
— George Bernard Shaw (1856-1950),
Irish-English playwright, music critic, wit

CROSBY, BING

He was an average guy who could carry a tune.
> – "Bing" (Harry Lillis) Crosby (1903-77),
> American singer, actor, comedian
> jokingly suggesting his own epitaph,
> quoted in *Newsweek* (Oct. 1977)

Oh, the kinda singing I do, you can't hurt your voice.
> – "Bing" (Harry Lillis) Crosby (1903-77),

There is nothing in the world I wouldn't do for [Bob] Hope, and there is nothing he wouldn't do for me. ... We spend our days doing nothing for each other.
> – "Bing" (Harry Lillis) Crosby (1903-77),
> quoted in *The Observer* (May 1950)

I don't know the key to success, but the key to failure is trying to please everybody.
> – "Bing" (Harry Lillis) Crosby (1903-77),

CUCKOO

Sumer is icumen in,
Lhude sing cuccu!
Groweth sed, and bloweth med,
And springeth the wude nu –
Sing cuccu!

> – Anon.
> *Cuckoo Song* (ca. 1250)

Winter is icumen in,
Lhude sing Goddamm,
Raineth drop and staineth slop,
And how the wind doth ramm!
Sing: Goddamm.
Skiddeth bus and sloppeth us,

An ague hath my ham.
Freezeth river, turneth liver,
Damn you, sing: Goddamm.
Goddamm, Goddamm, 'tis why I am, Goddamm,
So 'gainst the winter's balm.
Sing goddamm, damm, sing Goddamm.
Sing goddamm, sing goddamm, DAMM.

> – Ezra Pound (1885-1972),
> American poet, philosopher, writer
> *Ancient Music* from *Uncollected Miscellaneous Poems*, (1902)

CULTURE

Culture may even be described simply as that which makes life worth living.

> – T. S. Eliot (1888-1965),
> American poet, writer,
> *Notes Towards a Definition of Culture* (1948)

When I hear anyone talk of culture, I reach for my revolver.

> – Hanns Johst (1890-1978), German playwright
> often attributed to Hermann Goering (1893-1946),
> Air Marshall in Nazi Germany

When you learn something from people, or from a culture, you accept it as a gift, and it is your lifelong commitment to preserve it and build on it.

> – Yo-Yo Ma (b.1955),
> French-American cellist

Culture is what your butcher would have if he were a surgeon.

> – Mary Pettibone Poole,
> English writer,
> *A Glass Eye at a Keyhole* (1938)

DANCE

O body swayed to music,
O brightening glance
How can we know
the dancer from the dance?

> – William Butler Yeats (1865-1939),
> Irish poet, playwright,
> *Among School Children* (1927)

The trouble with nude dancing is that not everything stops when the music stops.

> – Sir Robert Helpmann (1909-86),
> Australian dancer-choreographer,
> on the nude musical *Oh! Calcutta!* (1972)

They dance best who dance with desire.

> – Irving (Israel Lazarovitch) Layton (b.1912),
> Romanian-Canadian poet, writer
> *For Mao tse-Tung: A Meditation on Flies and Kings*

A Dance to the Music of Time

> – Anthony Powell (1905-200),
> English novelist,
> title of a novel sequence (1951-75)

DARKNESS

For me, singing sad songs often has a way of healing a situation. It gets the hurt out in the open into the light, out of the darkness.

> – Reba McEntire (b.1955),
> American country singer-songwriter

DAUGHTERS

And the doors shall be shut in the streets, when the sound of
the grinding is low, and he shall rise up at the voice of the
bird, and all the daughters of music shall be brought low.
> – *Ecclesiastes* 12:1-4

DEATH

Susanna's music touched the bawdy strings
Of those white elders; but, escaping,
Left only Death's ironic scraping.
Now, in its immortality, it plays
On the clear viol of her memory,
And makes a constant sacrament of praise.
> – Wallace Stevens (1879-1955),
> American poet, writer,
> *Peter Quince at the Clavier* (1923)

On my gravestone, I want it to
say, 'I told you I was sick.'
> – Tom Waits (b.1949),
> American singer-songwriter

DEATHLESS

Out of me unworthy and
unknown
The vibrations of deathless
music
> – Edgar Lee Masters (1869-1950),
> American poet, writer,
> *Spoon River Anthology:*
> *Anne Rutledge*

DEBUSSY, CLAUDE

I have already heard it. I had better not go: I will start to get
accustomed to it and finally like it.
> – Nikolai Rimsky-Korsakov (1844-1908),
> Russian composer,
> on a concert of French composer Claude Debussy's music

DELIUS, FREDERICK

The musical equivalent of blancmange.
> – Bernard Levin, (b.1928)
> English writer, critic, wit,
> on English composer Frederick Delius (1862-1934)

DESPAIR

Action is the antidote to despair.
> – Joan Baez (b.1941),
> American singer-songwriter, activist

DIMINISHED SEVENTH

The diminished seventh provides access to any one of the
four major or four minor keys: Samuel Butler called it the
Clapham Junction of the keyboard.
> – Anthony Burgess (1917-93),
> English novelist, composer,
> *This Man and Music* (1983)

DISCO

Disco dancing is ... just the steady thump of a giant moron knocking in an endless nail.

— Clive James (b.1939),
Australian writer, journalist, critic, wit
in the London *Sunday Observer* (Dec. 1978)

DISCORD

Music, to create harmony, must investigate discord.

— Plutarch (ca 45-125),
Greek philosopher,
Lives: Demetrius

How shall we find the concord of this discord?

— William Shakespeare (1564-1616),
English poet, playwright,
Theseus, in *A Midsummer Night's Dream*,
act 5, scene 1, line 60

DJs

I am amazed at radio DJs today. I am firmly convinced that AM on my radio stands for Absolute Moron. I will not begin to tell you what FM stands for.

— Jasper Carrott (b.1945),
English comedian, musician, writer,

DOWLAND, JOHN

If music and sweet poetry agree,
As they must needs, the sister and the brother,
Then must the love be great 'twixt thee and me,
Because thou lovest the one, and I the other.
Dowland to thee is dear, whose heavenly touch
Upon the lute doth ravish human sense;
Spenser to me, whose deep conceit is such
As, passing all conceit, needs no defence.
Thou lovest to hear the sweet melodious sound
That Phoebus' lute, the queen of music, makes;
And I in deep delight am chiefly drown'd
When as himself to singing he betakes.
One god is god of both, as poets feign;
One knight loves both, and both in thee remain.
— William Shakespeare (1564-1616),
The Passionate Pilgrim, verse 8, on English lutenist
and songwriter John Dowland (1562-1626)

DREAMS

We are the music-makers,
And we are the dreamers of dreams.
— Arthur William Edgar O'Shaugnessy (1844-81),
English poet, writer,
Ode

DRUGS

Boy, you could be the greatest guitar player that ever lived,
but you won't live to see 40 if you don't leave that white
powder alone.
— B.B. (Riley) King (b.1925), American blues guitarist, singer-
songwriter to fellow blues guitarist Stevie Ray Vaughn
(1954-90) on Vaughn's cocaine habit. (King was
half-right: Vaughn didn't live to see 40,
as he died in a helicopter crash.)

The drug-abusing sex maniac part is true. The drug of choice is marijuana.

> – Ashley MacIsaac (b.1974),
> Canadian musician, fiddler, on rumors of his lifestyle,
> quoted in the *National Post*(April 2003)

Let's just say that you reach a stage in your life where you are curious. And I was curious at one point. But I'm way too focused to let anything stop me. Was it a mistake? Yes.

> – Britney Spears (b.1981),
> American singer, performer,
> on experimenting with drugs

Everything's better when you're straight, except fucking up.

> – Deborah Harry (b.1945),
> American singer-songwriter, performer (Blondie)

DRUMMER

If a man does not keep pace with his companion, perhaps it is because he hears a different drummer. Let him step to the music which he hears, however measured or far away.

> – Henry David Thoreau (1817-62),
> American writer, philosopher, poet,
> *Walden* (1854)

DYING

Let me have music dying, and I seek
No more delight

> – John Keats (1795-1821),
> English poet, *Endymion* (1818)

DYNAMICS

We're working with dynamics now. We've spent two years
with loud, and we've spent six months with deafening.

> – Jerry Garcia (1942-95),
> American musician, singer-songwriter (The Grateful Dead),
> quoted in *Popular Song and Youth Today* (1971)

EAR

I have a reasonable good ear in music: let us have the tongs
and the bones.

> – William Shakespeare (1564-1616),
> English poet, playwright,
> Bottom, in *A Midsummer Night's Dream*, act 4, scene 1, line 28

Because I have no ear for music, at the concert of the
Quintette Club, it looked to me as if the performers were
crazy, and the the audiences were make-believe crazy, and
all the audience were make-believe crazy, in order to soothe
the lunatics and keep them amused.

> – Ralph Waldo Emerson (1803-82),
> American philosopher, essayist, poet,
> *Journals*

He has Van Gogh's ear for music.

> Billy Wilder, (1906-2002)
> Polish-American film director,
> on actor Cliff Osmond (b.1937)

EISENHOWER, DWIGHT D.

Fourteen heart attacks and he had to die in my week. In *my*
week!

> – Janis Joplin (1943-70), American singer-songwriter,
> when the death of former U.S. president
> Dwight D. Eisenhower (1890-1969) bumped her picture off
> the cover of *Newsweek* magazine, quoted in
> *New Musical Express* (April 1969)

Elgar, Sir Edward

Holy water in a German beer barrel.

> – George Moore,
> American writer, critic
> on *The Dream of Gerontius* (1900),
> by English composer Sir Edward Elgar (1857-1934)

Emotions

I realized that while I'm not happy with things that are out of my control – like the state of the world, or the health of the planet – I do have a lot to celebrate on a personal level. Unless I allow myself to do that, I'm just going to make myself sick with all the heartache. I can still do my part, but I can't take everything on in such an emotional way.

> – Chantal Kreviazuk (b.1974)
> Canadian singer-songwriter,
> quoted in *Inside Entertainment* (Dec, 2002)

England

You that love England, who have an ear for her music,
The slow movement of clouds in benediction,
Clear arias of light thrilling over her uplands,
Over the chords of summer sustained peacefully

> – Cecil Day-Lewis (1904-72),
> English poet, writer,
> *Magnetic Mountain* (1933)

Epigram

Epigram: A wisecrack that played Carnegie Hall.

> – Oscar Levant (1906-72),
> American pianist, composer,
> *Coronet* (September 1958)

Eunuch

Eunuch: A man who has had his works cut out for him.
— Robert Byrne,
American writer, lexicographer

Experience

Music is your own experience, your own thoughts, your wisdom. If you don't live it, it won't come out of your horn. They teach you there's a boundary line to music. But, man, there's no boundary line to art.
— Charlie "Bird" Christopher Parker Jr. (1920–1955),
American jazz musician, composer
quoted in *Children of Albion: Poetry of the Underground in Britain*, ed. Michael Horovitz (1969)

Exquisite

When she had passed, it seemed like
the ceasing of exquisite music
— Henry Wadsworth Longfellow (1807-82),
English poet,
Evangeline (1847)

Eyes

Music that gentlier on the spirit lies,
Than tir'd eyelids upon tired eyes.
> – Alfred Lord Tennyson (1809-92),
> English poet,
> *The Lotus-Eaters: Choric Song* (1832)

Face

Oh, could you view the melody
Of every grace
And music of her face,
You'd drop a tear;
Seeing more harmony
In her bright eye
Than now you hear
> – Richard Lovelace (1618-58),
> English poet
> *Lucasta: Orpheus to Beasts* (1649)

Fame

Sometimes it's like you're a big pie settin' on the table, and everybody runs up and gets their piece of you. When it's over, the plate's empty.
> – Loretta Lynn (b.1935),
> American country singer-songwriter

It's nice to be so big that people who hate us stand outside in the cold to tell us they hate us.
> – Steve Jocz (b.1981),
> Canadian musician (Sum 41),
> quoted in the *National Post* (2003)

FENCE

Oh, give me land, lots of land
Under starry skies above,
Don't fence me in

> – Cole Porter (1891-1964),
> American songwriter, composer,
> *Don't Fence Me In* (song)

FIDDLE

He could fiddle all the bugs off a sweet potato vine.
> – Stephen Vincent Benét (1898-1943),
> American writer, poet,
> *The Mountain Whippoorwill* (1923)

Perhaps it was because Nero played the fiddle, they burned Rome.
> – Oliver Herford (1863-1935),
> English-American writer, humorist

He was a fiddler, and consequently a rogue.
> – Jonathan Swift (1667-1745),
> Irish-English writer, satirist, clergyman,
> testifying to a judge on the character of a prisoner

FILM MUSIC

Film music should have the same relationship to the film drama that somebody's piano playing in my living room has to the book I am reading.
> – Igor Stravinsky (1882–1971),
> Russian-American composer,
> quoted in *Music Digest* (Sept. 1946)

A [film] musician is like a mortician. He can't bring a body to life, but he can make it look better.
> – Adolf Deutsch (1897-1980),
> English-American composer,

FINE ARTS

Music must take rank as the highest of the fine arts – as the one which, more than any other, ministers to human welfare.
> – Herbert Spencer (1820-1903),
> English philosopher, writer
> *Essays on Education: On the Origin and Function of Music*
> (1861)

FLATTERY

Music's golden tongue
Flattered to tears this aged man and poor;
> – John Keats (1795–1821),
> English poet,
> *The Eve of St. Agnes*

FLED

Was it a vision, or a waking dream?
Fled is that music: – Do I wake or sleep?
> – John Keats (1795-1821),
> English poet,
> *Ode to a Nightingale* (1819)

FLUTE

A tutor who tooted the flute
Tried to tutor two tooters to toot.
Said the two to the tutor,
"Is it harder to toot or
To tutor two tooter to toot?"

> – Anon.

The soft complaining flute,
In dying notes, discovers
The woes of helpless lovers.
> – John Dryden (1631-1700),
> English poet, writer
> *A Song for St. Cecilia's Day* (1687),
> set to music by G.F. Handel (1685-1758)

Of all musicians, flautists are most obviously the ones who know something we don't know.
> – Paul Jennings (b.1918),
> English humorist, writer,
> *Flautists Flaunt Afflatus, The Jenguin Pennings* (1963)

Folk Music

All music is folk music. I ain't never heard no horse sing a song.
> – Louis "Satchmo" Armstrong (1901-71),
> American jazz musician, singer-songwriter

The only thing to do with a folk melody, once you have played it, is to play it louder.
> – Anon.

The farmer's daughter hath soft brown hair
(Butter and eggs and a pound of cheese);
And I met a ballad, I can't say where
Which wholly consisted of lines like these.
> – C.S. Calverley (1831-84),
> English poet,
> *Ballad*

I should like to consider the folk song, and expound briefly on a theory I have held for some time, to the effect that the reason most folk songs are so atrocious is that they were written by the people. If professional songwriters had written them instead, things might have turned out considerably differently.
> – Tom Lehrer (b.1928),
> American singer-songwriter, mathematician,
> introducing his arrangement of *Clementine*, recorded in
> concert at Sanders Theater, Harvard University (Mar, 1959)

A folksinger is someone who sings through his nose by ear.
> – Anon.

You have to admire people who sing [a protest song.] It takes a certain amount of courage to get up in a coffeehouse or a college auditorium and come out in favor of the things that everybody else in the audience is against, like peace and justice and brotherhood, and so on. The nicest thing about a protest song is that it makes you feel so good. I have a song here which I realize should be accompanied on a folk instrument – in which category the piano does not, alas, qualify. So imagine, if you will, that I am playing an 88-string guitar.

–Tom Lehrer (b.1928),
American singer-songwriter, mathematician,
introducing his song *The Folk Song Army*,
recorded at the 'hungry i', San Francisco (1965)

We are The Folk Song Army,
Every one of us cares,
We all hate poverty, war and injustice
— unlike the rest o' you squares.
...
If you feel dissatisfaction,
Strum your frustrations away.
Some people may prefer action, but
Gimme a folk song, any old day.

The tune don't have to be clever,
And it don't matter if you put a coupla extra syllables
into a line.
It sounds more ethnic if it ain't good English
And it don't even gotta rhyme.
(Excuse me — Rhine.)

Remember the war against Franco,
That's the kind where each of us belongs.
Though he may have won all the battles,
We had all the good songs. ...
So join in The Folk Song Army,
Guitars are the weapons we bring
To the fight against poverty, war and injustice.
Ready ... Aim ... Sing!

> –Tom Lehrer (b.1928),
> American singer-songwriter, mathematician,
> *The Folk Song Army*, recorded at the 'hungry i,'
> San Francisco (1965)

FRIEND

And the song, from beginning to end,
I found in the heart of a friend

> – Henry Wadsworth Longfellow (1807-82),
> English poet,
> *The Arrow and the Song* (1845)

FUGUE

To the average Briton the fugue is still an acute phase of a disease of dullness which occasionally breaks out in drawing rooms, and is known there as classical music.

> – George Bernard Shaw (1856-1950),
> Irish-English playwright, music critic, wit
> *Fugue Out of Fashion,*
> in *The Magazine of Music* (Nov. 1885)

So you want to write a fugue,
You have the urge to write a fugue,
You have the nerve to write a fugue
So go ahead

> – Glenn Gould (1932-82)
> Canadian musician, pianist, composer,
> *So You Want to Write a Fugue*

Learn thoroughly how to compose a fugue, and then *don't*.
— George Bernard Shaw (1856-1950),
Irish-English playwright, music critic, wit
Fugue Out of Fashion,
in *The Magazine of Music* (Nov. 1885)

As any musician will tell you, there is only one thing to do when you wake at five, and that is to compose a fugue. ... God knows why I am writing fugues. It is certainly not to waken the sleeping soul of Bach. Fugue is something that gets into you and, when one has composed forty-eight of the bastards, flies, or fugues, out again.
— Anthony Burgess (1917-93),
English novelist, composer,
in his preface to *Bach, Beethoven and the Boys* (1986)

FUNERAL MUSIC

Very nice, but tell me frankly, don't you think it would have been better if it had been *you* who had died, and your *uncle* who had written the *Funeral March?*
— attributed to Gioacchino Rossini (1792-1868),
Italian composer,
on being shown funeral music for
Giacomo Meyerbeer (1791-1864),
composed by Meyerbeer's nephew

GERSHWIN, GEORGE

The European boys have small ideas but they sure know how to dress 'em up.

> – George Gershwin (1898-1937),
> American composer,
> on the music of French composer
> Arthur Honneger (1892-1955)

George [Gershwin] died on July 11, 1937, but I don't have to believe that if I don't want to.

> – John O'Hara (1905-70),
> American writer,
> in *Newsweek* (July 1940)

GOD

If only God would give me some clear sign! Like making a large deposit in my name at a Swiss bank.

> – Woody (Allen Stewart Konigsberg) Allen (b.1935),
> American filmmaker, actor, comic, jazz musician

Not only is there no God, but try finding a plumber on Sunday.

> – Woody (Allen Stewart Konigsberg) Allen (b.1935),
> American filmmaker, actor, comic, jazz musician

The God of Music dwelleth out of doors.

> – Edith Matilda Thomas (1854-1925),
> American poet

I only answer to two people – myself and God.

> – Cher (Cherilyn Lapierre) (b.1946),
> American singer-songwriter, actress, performer

God tells me how the music should sound, but you stand in the way!

> – Arturo Toscanini (1867-1957),
> Italian conductor,
> reprimanding a trumpet player

This music of yours. A manifestation of the highest energy — not at all abstract, but without an object, energy in a void, in pure ether — where else in the universe does such a thing appear? We Germans have taken over from philosophy the expression 'in itself,' we use it every day without much idea of the metaphysical. But here you have it, such music is energy itself, yet not as idea, rather in its actuality. I call your attention to the fact that is almost the definition of God. *Imitatio Dei* — I am surprised it is not forbidden.

– Thomas Mann (1875–1955),
German writer, critic,
Doktor Faustus (1947, 1954)

The music, yearning like a God in pain.

– John Keats (1795-1821),
English poet,
Poems: The Eve of St. Agnes (1820)

Why attack God? He may be as miserable as we are.

– Erik Satie (1866-1925),
French composer

The German imagines even God is a singer.

– Friedrich Nietszche (1844-1900),
German philospher, writer

GOOD

One and the same thing can at the same time be good, bad, and indifferent, e.g., music is good to the melancholy, bad to those who mourn, and neither good nor bad to the deaf.

– Baruch Spinoza (1632-77),
Dutch philosopher, writer,
Ethics (1677)

GRAMMY

The Grammy was just the final stroke of a year of change. Winning the Grammy just meant that the phone rang a lot more.

– Jesse Harris (b.1970),
American singer-songwriter,
on winning a Grammy with Norah Jones
for *Don't Know Why*, quoted in *The Globe and Mail*
(May 2003)

GRIEFS

Where griping griefs the heart would wound
And doleful dumps the mind oppress,
There music with her silver sound
With speed is wont to send redress

– Anon.
A Song to the Lute in Musicke (circa 1600)

GUITAR

I look at you all,
See the love there that's sleeping
While my guitar gently weeps.

– George Harrison (1943-2001),
English musician singer-songwriter, (The Beatles),
While My Guitar Gently Weeps (1968)

HAPPINESS

We have no more right to consume happiness without producing it than to consume wealth without producing it.
— George Bernard Shaw (1856-1950),
Irish-English playwright, music critic, wit,
Candida (1898)

HARMONY

How sweet the moonlight sleeps upon this bank!
Here will we sit, and let the sound of music
Creep in our ears. Soft stillness and the night
Become the touches of sweet harmony.
Sit, Jessica. Look how the floor of heaven
Is thick inlaid with patens of bright gold.
There's not the smallest orb which thou behold'st
But in his motion like an angel sings,
Still quiring to the young-ey'd cherubins;
Such harmony is in immortal souls,
But whilst this muddy vesture of decay
Doth grossly close it in, we cannot hear it.
— William Shakespeare (1564-1616),
English poet, playwright,
Lorenzo, in *The Merchant of Venice*,
act 5, scene 1, lines 54-65

Here lyes Henry Purcell Esqre, who left Lyfe and is gone to that Blessed Place where only his harmony can be exceeded.
— epitaph for Henry Purcell (1659-95),
English composer, buried in Westminster Abbey

O but they say the tongues of dying men
Enforce attention like deep harmony.
— William Shakespeare (1564-1616),
English poet, playwright,
John of Gaunt, in *Richard II*,
act 2, scene 1, line 5

Untwisting all the chains that tie
The hidden soul of harmony.

> — John Milton (1608-74),
> English poet,
> *L'Allegro* (1632)

Beauty is harmony, grace is melody.

> — Juan Montalvo (1832-89),
> Ecuadorean essayist, political writer,
> *On Beauty*

Dust as we are, the immortal spirit grows
Like harmony in music; there is a dark
Inscrutable workmanship that reconciles
Discordant elements, makes them cling together
In one society.

> — William Wordsworth (1770-1850),
> English poet,
> *The Prelude*

HARP

The harp that once through Tara's halls
The soul of music shed,
Now hangs as mute on Tara's walls
As if that soul were fled.

> — Thomas Moore (1779-1852),
> Irish poet, writer,
> *The Harp That Once Through Tara's Halls*

Harpists spend 90 per cent of their lives tuning their harps
and 10 per cent playing out of tune.

> — Igor Stravinsky (1882-1971),
> Russian-American composer

HARPSICHORD

Two skeletons copulation on a corrugated tin roof.
– Sir Thomas Beecham (1879-1961),
English conductor

The sound of the harpsichord resembles that of a birdcage
played with a toasting-fork.
– Sir Thomas Beecham (1879-1961),
English conductor

A scratch with a sound at the end of it.
– definition of a harpsichord,
quoted by Percy A. Scholes (1877-1958),
English writer, broadcaster, educator
in *The Oxford Companion to Music*

HAYDN, FRANZ JOSEPH

Haydn had neither the flashy individuality of Mozart nor
the brooding, romantic passion of Beethoven. He was more
of a middle-management type.
– David W. Barber (b.1958),
Canadian journalist, humorist, musician,
Bach, Beethoven and the Boys (1986)

HEARING

To listen is an effort, and just to hear is no merit. A duck
hears also.
– Igor Stravinsky (1882-1971),
Russian-American composer

HEART

The music in my heart I bore
Long after it was heard no more.
— William Wordsworth (17710-1850),
English poet,
The Solitary Reaper (1803)

HEAVEN

The sweetest music this side of heaven.
— slogan of Guy (Gaetano Alber) Lombardo (1902-77),
Canadian bandleader, performer

HIPPIES

The hippies wanted peace and love. We wanted Ferraris,
blondes and switchblades.
— Alice (Vincent Furnier) Cooper (b.1948),
American musician, performer

HOMOSEXUALITY

If gays are granted rights, next we'll have to give rights to prostitutes and to people who sleep with St. Bernards and to nailbiters.

– Anita Bryant (b.1940),
American singer, crusader

HUMANITY

I always had a repulsive need to be something more than human.
– David (David Robert Jones) Bowie (b.1947),
English singer-songwriter, actor, performer

I have learned
To look on nature, not as in the hour
Of thoughtless youth; but hearing oftentimes
The still, sad music of humanity.

– William Wordsworth (1770-1850),
English poet,
Lines Composed a Few Miles Above Tintern Abbey (1798)

HUMILITY

I've never had a humble opinion. If you've got an opinion, why be humble about it?

– Joan Baez (b.1941),
American singer-songwriter, activist

HUMOR

A musician's humor is the inevitable distillation of a capacity to listen to himself, honestly to take blame for his own mistakes and shortcomings, a freedom from prejudice and an ability to see himself in as unreal and ludicrous a light

as others might see him, this extraterrestrial being –
messenger, clown, seer, priest or demon — exposing and
liberating us to ourselves in the deepest sense possible and
without the accusatory embarrassment of words. For humor
is the gift of the gods — born of deep humanity, of suffering
and compassion...
> – Sir Yehudi Menuhin (1916-1999),
> American-English, violinist, conductor, writer,
> in his preface to *A Musician's Dictionary* (1990)

Laughter is the shortest distance between two people.
> – Victor Borge (1909-2000),
> Danish-American musical humorist, pianist

IMMORTALITY

I don't want to achieve immortality through my work. ... I
want to achieve it through not dying.
> – Woody (Allen Stewart Konigsberg) Allen (b.1935),
> American filmmaker, actor, comic, jazz musician

INTELLECTUALS

Intellectuals should never marry; they might enjoy it; and
besides, they should not reproduce themselves.
> – Don Herold (1889-1966),
> American writer

INSPIRATION

Blessed Cecilia, appear in visions
To all musicians, appear and inspire:
Translated Daughter, come down and startle
Composing mortals with immortal fire.
> – W. H. Auden (1907-73),
> English poet, *Hymn to St. Cecilia* (1942),
> set to music by Sir Benjamin Britten (1913-77)

All the inspiration I ever needed was a phone call from a producer.
> – Cole Porter (1893-1964),
> American songwriter, composer

Nothing primes inspiration more than necessity, whether it be the presence of a copyist waiting for your work, or the prodding of an impresario tearing his hair. In my time, all the impresarios of Italy were bald at 30.
> – Gioacchino Rossini (1792-1868),
> Italian composer

INSTRUMENT(S)

Why, look you now, how unworthy a thing you make of me! You would play upon me; you would seem to know my stops; you would pluck out the heart of my mystery; you would sound me from my lowest note to the top of my compass: and there is much music, excellent voice, in this little organ; yet cannot you make it speak. 'Sblood, do you think I am easier to be played on than a pipe? Call me what instrument you will, though you can fret me, yet you cannot play upon me.
> – William Shakespeare (1564-1616),
> English poet, playwright,
> Hamlet, in *Hamlet*, act 3, scene 2

Since I am coming to that holy room,
Where, with thy choir of saints forevermore,
I shall be made thy music; as I come
I tune the instrument at the door,
And what I must do then, think here before.
> – John Donne (1573-1631),
> English poet, clergyman,
> *Hymn to God My God, in My Sickness*

INSULTS

No one can have a higher opinion of him than I have, and I think he's a dirty little beast.

– W. S. Gilbert (1836-1911),
English operetta librettist

INTERNATIONALISM

Music has always been transnational; people pick up whatever interests them, and certainly a lot of classical music has absorbed influences from all over the world.

– Yo-Yo Ma (b.1955),
French-American cellist

INVISIBLE

Music sets up ladders,
it makes us invisible,
it sets us apart,
it lets us escape;
but from the visible
there is no escape.

– Hilda Doolittle (1886–1961),
American poet,
Tribute to the Angels

JAZZ

Jazz is not about flat fives or sharp nines, or metric subdivisions, or substitute chord changes. Jazz is about feeling,communication, honesty, and soul. Jazz is not supposed to boggle the mind. Jazz is meant to enrich the spirit. Jazz can create jubilance. Jazz can induce melancholy. Jazz can energize. Jazz can soothe. Jazz can make you shake your head, clap your hands, and stomp your feet. Jazz can render you spellbound and hypnotized. Jazz can be soft or hard, heavy or light, cool or hot, bright or dark. Jazz is for your heart. Jazz moves you.

> – Joshua Redman (b.1969)
> American jazz musician,
> quoted in *Moodswing* (Apr, 1994)

If you have to ask what jazz is, you'll never know.

> – Louis "Satchmo" Armstrong (1901-71),
> American jazz musician, singer-songwriter, bandleader

Jazz will endure just as long as people hear it through their feet instead of their brains.

> – John Philip Sousa (1854-1932),
> American bandmaster, songwriter, composer

Madam, if you don't know by now, Dont Mess With It!!

> – "Fats" Thomas Waller (1904-43),
> American jazz pianist, singer-songwriter,bandleader
> asked to define jazz

If you see me up there on the stand smiling, I'm lost!

> – Earl "Fatha" Kenneth Hines (1903-83),
> American jazz pianist, singer-songwriter, bandleader

A jazz musician is a juggler who uses harmonies instead of oranges.

> – Benny Green (1927-98),
> English jazz musician, writer, broadcaster,
> *The Reluctant Art* (1962)

Epitaph for a tombstone of a cool musician: "Man, this cat is really gone."
>   – *More Playboy's Party Jokes* (1965)

By and large, jazz has always been like the kind of a man you wouldn't want your daughter to associate with.
>   – "Duke" (Edward Kennedy) Ellington (1889-1974),
>   American jazz pianist, composer, bandleader

Man, I can't *listen* that fast.
>   – Unnamed jazz musician, on hearing
>   Charlie Parker and Dizzy Gillespie's *Shaw Nuff.*

Playing 'bop' is like playing Scrabble with all the vowels missing.
>   – "Duke" (Edward Kennedy) Ellington (1889-1974),
>   American jazz pianist, composer, bandleader,
>   in *Look* magazine (Aug. 1954)

I'll play it first and tell you what it is later.
>   – Miles Dewey Davis (1926-91),
>   American jazz musician, composer, artist

That's just like tapping a nightingale on the shoulder, saying 'How's that again, dickey-bird?'
>   – Louis Armstrong to Danny Kaye, on why nobody
>   writes down Dixieland, in *The Five Pennies* (1959)

JESUS CHRIST

Christianity will go. It will vanish and shrink. I needn't argue about that: I'm right and I will be proved right. We're [the Beatles are] more popular than Jesus now. I don't know which will go first — rock 'n' roll or Christianity.
>   – John Lennon (1940-80),
>   English musician, singer-songwriter, (The Beatles),
>   quoted in *The Evening Standard* (March 1966)

Ernest, don't you think Al Jolson is greater than Jesus?
– Zelda Sayre Fitzgerald (1900-48),
American writer, novelist, (wife of novelist
F. Scott Fitzgerald, remark to American writer, novelist
Ernest Hemingway (1899-1961), quoted in
Hemingway's *A Moveable Feast* (1964)

KEYBOARD

The keyboard has never developed into a proper typewriter, for the alphabet is unmarked and in no case extends beyond the letter G, and it is further devoid of numerals. For these reasons pianists do not make successful secretaries.
– Sir Yehudi Menuhin (1916-1999),
American-English, violinist, conductor, writer,
in his preface to *A Musician's Dictionary* (1990)

KILLING

If it's natural to kill, how come men have to go into training to learn how?
– Joan Baez (b.1941),
American singer-songwriter, activist

KISS

You must remember this,
A kiss is still a kiss,
A sigh is just a sigh;
The fundamental things apply,
As time goes by
– Herman Hupfeld (1894-1951),
American songwriter, composer,
As Time Goes By (1931)

KNITTING

I write music as old women knit.
> – Anthony Burgess (1917-93),
> English novelist, composer,
> remark in a lecture, 1982. [Meaning he writes
> music as a way to pass the time, as a pleasant distraction,
> not that he composes while women knit in the background.]

KNOWLEDGE

We are here and it is now. Further than that all human knowledge is moonshine.
> – H.L. Mencken (1880-1956),
> American journalist, writer, music critic

LANGUAGE

What was the language of this symphony? A language altogether proper for a young man composing music in England in 1935. Diatonic, swift to modulate, inclined to the modal, Vaughan Williams harmonies, occasional tearing dissonances like someone farting at a teaparty, bland, meditative, with patches of vular triumph. Totally English music, hardly able to jump twenty-two miles into Europe.
> – Anthony Burgess (1917-93),
> English novelist, composer,
> on his *Symphony No. 1 in E major,*
> *This Man and Music* (1983)

Music is the universal language of mankind — poetry their universal pastime and delight.
> – Henry Wadsworth Longfellow (1807-1882),
> English poet,
> *Outre-Mer* (1833-34)

Music has often been compared with language itself, and the comparison is quite legitimate. While it combines easily with actual language, it also speaks a language of its own, which it has become a platitude to call universal. To understand the significance of the organizing factors of rhythm, melody, harmony, tone color and form, the analogy of a familiar language is helpful. Music has its own alphabet of only seven letters, as compared with the twenty-six of the English alphabet. Each of these letters represents a note, and just as certain letters are complete words in themselves, so certain notes may stand alone, with the force of a whole word. Generally, however, a note of music implies a certain harmony, and in most modern music the notes take the form of actual chords. So it may be said that a chord in music is analogous to a word in language. Several words form a phrase, and several phrases a complete sentence, and the same thing is true in music. Measured music corresponds to poetry, while the old unmeasured plain-song might be compared with prose.

– Sigmund Spaeth (1885–1965),
American musicologist, writer,
The Art of Enjoying Music (1933)

LEGEND(S)

A legend is an old man with a cane known for what he used to do. I'm still doing it.
– Miles Dewey Davis (1926-91),
American jazz musician,
composer, artist

LIBERACE

You know that bank I used to cry all the way to? I bought it.
— Liberace (Vladzin Valentino) Liberace (1919-87),
American pianist, performer (see *Criticism*, above)

LIBERTY

Liberty has never come from the government. Liberty has always come from the subjects of it. The history of liberty is a history of resistance. The history of liberty is a history of limitations of governmental power, not the increase of it.
— Nadia Boulanger (1887-1979),
French composer, conductor, teacher

LIFE

Life is what happens to you while you're busy making other plans.
— John Lennon (1940-80),
English musician, singer-songwriter, actor,
(The Beatles)

Life isn't fair. It's just fairer than death, that's all.
— William Goldman (b.1931),
American writer, screenwriter,
in *The Princess Bride* (1973)

Life is like playing a violin solo in public and learning the instrument as one goes along.
— Samuel Butler (1835-1902),
English poet, writer,
in a speech at the Somerville Club (Feb, 1895)

Oh, life is a glorious cycle of song,
A medley of extemporanea;

And love is a thing that can never go wrong;
And I am Marie of Roumania
– Dorothy Parker (1893-1967),
American writer, journalist,
Comment, in *Not So Deep as a Well* (1937)

Life is like a sewer: What you get out of it depends on what you put into it.
– Tom Lehrer (b.1928),
American singer-songwriter, mathematician,
in the preamble to his song
We Will All Go Together When We Go,
on *An Evening Wasted Wasted With Tom Lehrer* (1953)

LISTENING

The opposite of talking isn't listening. The opposite of talking is waiting.
– Fran Lebowitz (b.1950),
American journalist, writer,
Social Studies (1981)

LISZT, FRANZ

I know his mother only by correspondence, and one cannot arrange that sort of thing by correspondence.
– Franz Liszt (1811-86),
Hungarian composer, pianist,
on rumors that he fathered pianist Franz Servais

LLOYD WEBBER, SIR ANDREW

A confusing jamboree of piercing noise, routine roller-skating, misogyny and Orwellian special effects, *Starlight Express* is the perfect gift for the kid who has everything except parents.
– Frank Rich, *New York Times*,
a review of Sir Andrew Lloyd Webber's musical

LONELINESS

Music was invented to confirm human loneliness.

> – Lawrence Durrell (1912-90),
> Indian-English, writer
> in *Clea* (1960)

LOVE

Love me little, love me long,
Is the burden of my song.

> – Anon.,
> *Love Me Little* (ca. 1569)

Fain would I change that note
To which fond Love hath charmed me

> – from Tobias Hume (1569-1645)
> English composer, violinist,
> *Musical Humours* (1605)

If music be the food of love, play on;
Give me excess of it, that, surfeiting,
The appetite may sicken, and so die.
That strain again! It had a dying fall:
O, it came o'er my ear like the sweet sound,
That breathes upon a bank of violets,
Stealing and giving odor! Enough; no more:
'Tis not so sweet now as it was before.
— William Shakespeare (1564-1616),
English poet, playwright,
Duke Orsino, in *Twelfth Night*, act 1, scene 1

If music be the food of love,
Sing on till I am fill'd with joy;
For then my list'ning soul you move
To pleasures that can never cloy.
Your eyes, your mien, your tongue declare
That you are music ev'rywhere.
Pleasures invade both eye and ear,
So fierce the transports are, they wound,
And all my senses feasted are,
Tho' yet the treat is only sound,
Sure I must perish by your charms,
Unless you save me in your arms.
— Colonel Henry Heveningham,
in *Gentleman's Journal* (June, 1692),
(after Shakespeare, *Twelfth Night*) set
to music by Henry Purcell (1569-1695)

Give me some music; music, moody food
Of us that trade in love.
— William Shakespeare (1564-1616),
English poet, playwright,
Cleopatra, in *Anthony and Cleopatra*,
act 2, scene 5, line 1

In the end, the love you take is equal to the love you make.
— Sir Paul McCartney (b.1942),
English_musician, singer-songwriter, composer,
(The Beatles, Wings)

If music and sweet poetry agree,
As they must needs (the sister and the brother),
Then must the love be great 'twixt thee and me,
Because thou lov'st the one, and I the other.

– Richard Barnfield (1574–1629),
English poet,
To His Friend Master R.L., in Praise of Music and Poetry

Love is not the dying moan of a distant violin — it's the triumphant twang of a bedspring.

– S.J. Perelman (1904-79),
American writer, humorist

I sigh, I pine,
I squeak, I squawk.
Today I woke
too weak to walk.

– Stephen Sondheim (b.1930),
American lyricist, composer,
in *A Funny Thing Happened
on the Way to the Forum* (1962)

Birds do it, bees do it,
Even educated fleas do it.
Let's do it, let's fall in love

– Cole Porter (1891-1964),
American songwriter, composer
song, *Let's Do It* (1954)

All You Need is Love.

– John Lennon (1940-80) and Paul McCartney (b.1942),
English musicians, singer-songwriters, composers
(The Beatles), song title (1967)
Broadcast to the World via satellite
to over 150 million people worldwide.
Making it a number one hit

LOVERS

How silver-sweet sound lovers' tongues by night,
Like softest music to attending ears!
> – William Shakespeare (1564-1616),
> English poet, playwright,
> Romeo, in *Romeo and Juliet*,
> act 2, scene 2, lines 165-66

LUTE

My lute awake! perform the last
Labour that thou and I shall waste,
And end that I have now begun;
For when this song is sung and past,
My lute be still, for I have done
> – Sir Thomas Wyatt (1503-42),
> English poet,
> *My Lute Awake!*
> song (pub. 1557)

It is the little rift within the lute,
That by and by will make the music mute,
And ever widening slowly silence all.
> – Alfred Lord Tennyson (1809-92),
> English poet,
> *Idylls of the King: Merlin and Vivien* (1859-85)

MAD

This music mads me; let it sound no more.
— William Shakespeare (1564-1616),
English poet, playwright,
Richard, in *Richard II*, act 5, scene 5, line 61

I cried for madder music and for stronger wine.
— Ernest Dowson (1867-1900),
English poet,
Non Sum Qualis Eram Bonae Sub Regno Cynarae (1896)

MADONNA

Madonna shaved her legs to lose 30 pounds.
— Joan Rivers (b.1933),
American comedian, TV commentator

Everyone probably thinks that I'm a raving nymphomaniac, that I have an insatiable sexual appetite, when the truth is I'd rather read a book.

> – Madonna (Louise Ciccone) (b.1958),
> American singer-songwriter, performer, actress

[Madonna is] like a breast with a boom box.

> – Judy Tenuta (b.1956),
> American comedian

Michael keeps asking why I can't write songs like Madonna. I tell him because I have brains.

> – Cristina, English singer

Madonna and Sean Penn – beauty and the beast, but guess which one?

> – Joan Rivers (b.1933),
> American comedian, TV commentator

MAIDEN

I sing of a maiden
That is makéless;
King of all kings
To her son she ches.

> – Anon.
> carol, *I Sing of a Maiden* (15th century)

MASSENET, JULES

Massenet
Never wrote a Mass in A
It'd have been just too bad
If he had.

> – Anthony Butts, American poet,
> on French composer Jules Massenet (1842-1912)

McCartney, Sir Paul

Paul McCartney ... has become the oldest living cute boy in the world.

– Anna Quindlen,
American writer, journalist
New York Times

If slaughterhouses had glass walls, everyone would be a vegetarian.

– Sir Paul McCartney (b.1942),
English musician, singer-songwriter, composer,
(The Beatles, Wings)

Meaning

The whole problem can be stated quite simply by asking, Is there a meaning to music? My answer would be, Yes. And Can you state in so many words what the meaning is? My answer to that would be, No.

– Aaron Copland (1900-90),
American composer,
What to Listen For in Music (1939)

A Haydn symphony had a meaning for the social group which listened to it. A Mahler symphony had a meaning for the man who composed it. Here is the difference between the classical and romantic attitudes to art.

– Anthony Burgess (1917-93),
English novelist, composer,
This Man and Music (1983)

So long as the human spirit thrives on this planet, music in some living form will accompany and sustain it and give it expressive meaning.

– Aaron Copland (1900-90),
American composer,
quoted in the London *Times* (Nov. 1980)

MEDIOCRITY

It isn't evil that's ruining the Earth, but mediocrity. The crime is not that Nero played while Rome burned, but that he played badly.

> – Ned Rorem (b.1923),
> American composer, writer,
> *The Final Diary* (1974)

MELODY

Melody! The battle-cry of *dilettanti* !

> – Robert Schumann (1810-56),
> German composer

MEN AND WOMEN

I conclude that musical notes and rhythms were first acquired by the male or female progenitors of mankind for the sake of charming the opposite sex.

> – Charles Darwin (1766-1848),
> English scientist, writer,
> *The Descent of Man* (1871)

Instead of getting hard ourselves and trying to compete, women should try and give their best qualities to men— bring them softness, teach them how to cry.

> – Joan Baez (b.1941),
> American singer-songwriter, activist

I am fed up with men who use sex like a sleeping pill.

> – Toni Braxton (b.1967),
> American R&B singer-songwriter

A girl can wait for the right man to come along but in the meantime that still doesn't mean she can't have a wonderful time with all the wrong ones.

– Cher (Cherilyn Lapierre) (b.1946),
American singer-songwriter, actress, performer

Husbands are like fires — they go out when they're left unattended.

– Cher (Cherilyn Lapierre) (b.1946),
American singer-songwriter, actress, performer

It's true that I did get the girl, but then my grandfather always said, Even a blind chicken finds a few grains of corn now and then.

– Lyle Lovett (b.1956),
American country singer-songwriter,
on his brief marriage to film
actress Julia Roberts (b.1967)

MEMORY

The memory of things gone is important to a jazz musician. Things like old folks singing in the moonlight in the back yard on a hot night or something said long ago.

– Louis "Satchmo" Armstrong (1901-71),
American jazz musician, singer-songwriter, bandleader

MERRY

I am never merry when I hear sweet music.

– William Shakespeare (1564-1616),
English poet, playwright,
Jessica, in *The Merchant of Venice*,
act 5, scene 1, line 69

MEDICINE

The variable composition of man's body hath made it as an instrument easy to distemper. Therefore, the poets did well to conjoin music and medicine in Apollo, because the office of medicine is but to tune this curious harp of man's body and to reduce it to harmony.

> – Francis Bacon (1561-1626),
> English scientist, politician, writer,
> in *Advancement of Learning* (1605)

The Physitians will tell you that the exercise of Musicke is a great lengthener of life, by stirring and reviving of the Spirits, holding a secret sympathy with them.

> – Henry Peacham (1576-1643),
> English writer,
> in *The Compleat Gentleman* (1622)

Music's the medicine of the mind.

> – John Logan (1748-88),
> Scottish poet, writer,
> *Danish Ode* (1788)

MELANCHOLY

There was this strong sense of melancholy to the music —
not sadness, but a longing for your homeland or a loved one.
I really related to that, being away from Montreal.
> – Canadian musician, Stef (Stéphane) Carreau,
> on discovering Brazilian bossa nova music
> while studying in Paris in the 1980s,
> quoted in *Words & Music* (Summer 2003)

MELODY

A pretty girl is like a melody
That haunts you night and day
> – Irving (Israel Baline) Berlin, (1888-1989),
> Russian-American composer, pianist
> *A Pretty Girl is Like a Melody*,
> song (1919)

The song is ended (but the melody lingers on)
> – Irving (Israel Baline) Berlin (1888-1989),
> American composer,
> *The Song is Ended*,
> song (1927)

MEMPHIS

I remember going down to Beale Street when I was young
and listening to those voices coming out of those bars and
they were just soulful. It's the Bible Belt, so every church
choir in Memphis is a gospel choir, you know, whether you're
black, white, Mexican. It doesn't matter.
> – Justin Timberlake (b.1981),
> American singer, performer, actor,
> quoted in *Inside Entertainment* (July 2003)

MERCEDES-BENZ

Oh, Lord, won't you buy me
A Mercedes-Benz.
My friends all drive Porsches,
I must make amends
> – Janis Joplin (1943-70),
> American musician singer-songwriter,
> *Mercedes-Benz*,
> song (1970)

MERMAID(S)

Since once I sat upon a promontory,
And heard a mermaid on a dolphin's back
Uttering such dulcet and harmonious breath,
That the rude sea grew civil at here song,
And certain stars shot madly from their spheres
To hear the sea-maid's music.
> – William Shakespeare (1564-1616),
> English poet, playwright,
> Oberon, in *A Midsummer Night's Dream*,
> act 2, scene 1, lines 149-155

I have heard the mermaids singing, each to each
> – T.S. Eliot (1888-1965),
> American poet, writer,
> *Love Song of J. Alfred Prufrock* (1917)

MESSIAH

I should be sorry, my Lord, if I had only succeeded in entertaining them; I wished to make them better.
> – G.F. Handel (1685-1759),
> German-English composer,
> to Lord Kinnoull, after the first London
> performance of *Messiah* (Mar. 1743)

Come for tea. Come for tea, my people.

> – Anon.,
> parodying the opening tenor aria (*Comfort Ye*)
> in Handel's *Messiah*

Just a little more reverence, please, and not so much astonishment.

> – Sir Malcolm Sargent (1895-1967),
> English conductor,
> rehearsing a female chorus in
> *For Unto Us a Child Is Born*, from Handel's *Messiah*

MILITARY MUSIC

Military justice is to justice what military music is to music.

> – Julius "Groucho" Marx (1890-1977),
> American film comedic actor, writer

MIND

Music is the effort we make to explain to ourselves how our brains work. We listen to Bach transfixed because this is listening to a human mind.

> – Lewis Thomas (b.1913),
> American physician, writer,
> *On Thinking About Thinking*, in *The Medusa and the Snail*

The mind of man may be compared to a musical instrument with a certain range of notes, beyond which in both directions we have an infinitude of silence.

– John Tyndall (1820-93),
Irish surveyor, naturalist, scientist, educator,
*Fragments of Science, Vol. II:
Matter and Force* (1871)

Mistakes

It was when I found out I could make mistakes that I knew I was on to something.

– Ornette Coleman (b.1930),
American jazz musician, composer

When a musician hath forgot his note,
He makes as though a crumb
stuck in his throat

– John Clarke (d.1658),
Paroemiologia (1639)

Modern Music

I don't write modern music. I only write good music.

– Igor Stravinsky (1882-1971),
Russian-American composer

Three farts and a raspberry, orchestrated.

– Sir John Barbirolli,
English conductor,
describing modern music

My music is not modern, it is only badly played.

– Arnold Schoenberg (1874-1951),
Austrian-American composer

That's the worst of my reputation as a modern composer —
everyone must have thought I meant it.
                                    – Igor Stravinsky (1882-1971),
                                         Russian-American composer,
                                    on a misprint in one of his scores

MONEY

I don't care too much for money,
For money can't buy me love

                    – John Lennon (1940-80) and Paul McCartney (b.1942),
                         English musicians, singer-songwriters, composers
                                                        (The Beatles),
                                        song *Can't Buy Me Love*, (1964)

MOURNING

A tale out of season [is as] musick in mourning.
                                         – *Ecclesiasticus* 22:6

Most musical of mourners, weep again!
                                    – Percy Bysshe Shelley
                                              (1792-1822),
                                         English poet,
                                    Epipsychidion (1821)

MOZART, WOLFGANG AMADEUS

The *G-minor Symphony* consists of eight remarkable
measures ... surrounded by a half-hour of banality.
                                    – Glenn Gould (1932-82),
                         Canadian pianist, composer, broadcaster,
                                    on Mozart's *Symphony No. 40*,
                                    in *The Glenn Gould Reader* (1984)

I write as a sow piddles.
                    – Wolfgang Amadeus Mozart (1756-91),
                                   Austrian composer,
                                        in a letter

Ah, Mozart! He was happily married — but his wife wasn't.
                       – Victor Borge (1909-2000),
              Danish-American musical humorist, pianist

Nothing from Mozart?
                      – Sir Thomas Beecham (1879-1961),
                                  English conductor,
              on hearing his 70th-birthday telegrams

Mozart

There is no shadow of death anywhere in Mozart's music. Even his own funeral was a failure. It was dispersed by a shower of rain; and to this day nobody knows where he was buried or whether he was buried at all or not. My own belief is that he was not. Depend on it, they had no sooner put up their umbrellas and bolted for the nearest shelter than he got up, shook off his bones into the common grave of the people, and soared off into universality.
                      – George Bernard Shaw (1856-1950),
                     Irish-English playwright,
                           music critic, wit,
              Music in London, 1890-94 (1931)

Mozart is just God's way of making the rest of us feel insignificant.
                      – David W. Barber (b.1958),
              Canadian journalist, humorist,
              musician, in *Bach, Beethoven and the Boys* (1986)

It's people like that who make you realize how little you've
accomplished. It is a sobering thought, for example, that
when Mozart was my age — he had been dead for two years!

– Tom Lehrer (b.1928),
American singer-songwriter, mathematician,
on Alma Mahler Gropius Werfel,
in the preamble to his song *Alma*

MTV

MTV is the lava lamp of the 1980s.

– Doug Ferrari (b.1956),
American comedian

When I was young we didn't have MTV. We had to take
drugs and go to concerts.

– Steven Pearl,
American comedian

MUD

Mud! Mud! Glorious Mud!
Nothing quite like it
For cooling the blood

– Michael Flanders (1922-75),
English singer-comedic lyricist, pianist, writer,
Hippopotamus Song (1952)

MUSIC AND MUSICIANS

We shall never become musicians unless we understand the ideals for temperance, fortitude, liberality and magnificence.
— Plato (ca. 428-347 BC),
Greek philosopher

Music exults each joy, allays each grief,
Expels diseases, softens every pain,
Subdues the rage of poison and the plague
— John Armstrong (1709-79),
Scottish poet, physician,
The Art of Preserving Health (1744)

Music is enough for a lifetime — but a lifetime is not enough for music.
— Sergei Rachmaninoff (1873-1943),
Russian composer

There's a lot of great music out there and always has been. People just don't know about it sometimes. It's not that they're stupid. It's just that they get used to getting spoon-fed stuff by MTV and the media. They forget that you can't always trust that avenue of information. You've got to go out and find it sometimes.
— Norah Jones (b.1979),
American singer-songwriter,
quoted in *Inside Entertainment* (July 2003)

[A piece of music is] a code that opens a door to a world everybody interprets differently, because our aesthetic and sensory values are different and each generation has to discover its own.
— Yo-Yo Ma (b.1955),
French-American cellist

Without music, I could not get through.
                              – Shawn Colvin (b.1958),
                           American singer-songwriter

Music is another lady that talks charmingly and says
nothing.
                              – Austin O'Malley (1858-1932),
                                      American writer

I was born with music inside me. Music was one of my parts.
Like my ribs, my kidneys, my liver, my heart. Like my blood.
It was a force already within me when I arrived on the scene.
It was a necessity for me — like food or water.
                    – Ray (Ray Charles Robinson) Charles (b.1930),
             American jazz pianist, composer singer-songriter

I think music in itself is healing. It's an explosive expression
of humanity. It's something we are all touched by. No matter
what culture we're from, everyone loves music.
                              – Billy Joel (b.1949),
             American singer-songwriter, composer, pianist

Somehow you can tell the difference when a song is written
just to get on the radio and when what someone does is their
whole life. That comes through in [Bob] Dylan, Paul Simon,
Willie Nelson. There is no separating their life from their
music.
                              – Lyle Lovett (b.1956),
                     American country singer-songwriter

Music to hear, why hear'st thou music sadly?
Sweets with sweets war not, joy delights in joy,
Why lov'st thou that which thou receiv'st not gladly?
Or else receiv'st with pleasure thine annoy?
If the true concord of well-tuned sounds

By unions married, do offend thine ear,
They do but sweetly chide thee, who confounds
In singleness the parts that thou shouldst bear.
Mark how one string, sweet husband to another,
Strikes each in each by mutual ordering;
Resembling sire and child and happy mother,
Who, all in one, one pleasing note do sing;
Whose speechless song, being many, seeming one,
Sings this to thee, 'thou single wilt prove none.'

– William Shakespeare (1564-1616),
English poet, playwright,
Sonnet VIII

Music heard so deeply
That it is not heard at all, but you are
the music
While the music lasts.

– T.S. Eliot (1888-1965),
American poet, writer,
*Four Quartets: The Dry
Salvages* (1941)

Only sick music makes
money today.
– Friedrich Nietzsche
(1844-1900),
German philosopher,
writer (1888)

Music is essentially
useless, as is life.
– George Santayana
(1863-1952),
Spanish-American
philosopher, writer

Music is but a fart that's sent
From the guts of an instrument.

> – Anon.,
> *Wit and Drollery*, 1645

Too many pieces [of music] finish too long after the end.
> – Igor Stravinsky (1882-1971),
> Russian-American composer

Music with dinner is an insult both to the cook and the violinist.
> – G.K. Chesterton (1874-1936),
> English writer, critic

I know I have to beat time when I learn music. Ah! That accounts for it, said the Hatter. He won't stand beating.
> – Lewis (Charles Lutwidge Dodgson) Carroll (1832-98),
> English writer, mathematician,
> 'Alice and the Mad Hatter',
> in *Alice's Adventures in Wonderland* (1865)

The English may not like music — but they absolutely love the noise it makes.
> – Sir Thomas Beecham (1879-1961),
> English conductor,
> in the *New York Herald Tribune* (Mar, 1961)

My music is best understood by children and animals.
> – Igor Stravinsky (1882-1971),
> Russian-American composer

We often feel sad in the presence of music without words; and often more than that in the presence of music without music.
> – Mark (Samuel Langhorne Clemens) Twain (1835-1910),
> American writer, wit

I hate music, especially when it's played.
> – Jimmy Durante (1893-1980),
> American comedian, actor

When you are about 35 years old, something terrible happens to music.
>
> – Steve Race,
> remark on BBC Radio (1982)

MUSIC HALL

The other evening, feeling rather in want of a headache, I bethought me that I had not been to a music hall for a long time.
>
> – George Bernard Shaw (1856-1950),
> Irish-English playwright, music critic, wit

MUSICALS

The hills are alive — and it's rather frightening!
>
> – Anon.,
> parodying Rodgers and Hammerstein's
> *The Sound of Music.*

MUSICOLOGY

A musicologist is a man who can read music but can't hear it.

– Sir Thomas Beecham (1879-1961),
English conductor

MUZAK

Muzak goes in one ear and out some other opening.

– Anton Kuerti (b.1938),
Austrian-Canadian pianist,
quoted by Ulla Colgrass
in *For the Love of Music* (1988)

MUSIC BUSINESS

Music is spiritual. The music business is not.

– Van Morrison (b.1945),
Irish musician, singer-songwriter,
quoted in the London *Times* (July, 1990)

NATURE

There is a pleasure in the pathless woods,
There is a rapture on the lonely shore,
There is society, where none intrudes,
By the deep sea, and music in its roar:
I love not man the less, but Nature more.

– Lord (George Gordon) Byron (1788-1824),
English poet, writer,
Childe Harold's Pilgrimage, (1812)

For the Romantic composer Nature was not merely a subject to be depicted. A kinship was felt between the inner life of the artist and the life of Nature, so that the latter became not only a refuge but also a source of strength, inspiration, and revelation. This mystic sense of kinship with Nature, counterbalancing the artificiality of city existence, is a prevalent in the music of the nineteenth century as it is in the contemporary literature and art.

– Donald J. Grout (1902-87),
American music historian, writer,
A History of Western Music (1973)

The history of Western music has had much to do with the progressively making explicit of what nature leaves implicit.

– Anthony Burgess (1917-93),
English novelist, composer,
This Man and Music (1983)

NEIGHBORS

Every time I open a newspaper, I am reminded that we live in a world where we can no longer afford not to know our neighbors.

– Yo-Yo Ma (b.1955),
French-American cellist

NIGHT

And the night shall be filled with music,
And the cares, that infest the day,
Shall fold their tents, like the Arabs,
And as silently steal away.

> – Henry Wadsworth Longfellow (1807-82),
> English poet,
> *The Day is Done* (1845)

NIGHTINGALE

Except I be by Sylvia in the night,
There is no music in the nightingale.

> – William Shakespeare (1564-1616),
> English poet, playwright,
> Valentine, in *The Two Gentlemen of Verona*,
> act 3, scene 1, line 178

NOISE

What we know as modern music is the noise made by deluded
speculators picking through the slagpile.

> Henry Pleasants
> (1911-2000),
> American-English music critic, journalist,
> writer, spy,
> *The Agony of Modern Music* (1955)

As it enters the ear, does it come in like broken glass or does it come in like honey?
> – Eddie Condon (1905-73),
> American jazz musician

Music is the only noise for which one is obliged to pay.
> – Alexandre Dumas (1802-70),
> French writer (attrib.)

Music is the most disagreeable and the most widely beloved of all noises.
> – Théophile Gautier (1811-72)
> French poet, writer,
> in *Le Figaro* (Oct, 1863)

Of all noises, I think music is the least disagreeable.
> – Samuel Johnson (1709-84),
> English diarist, lexicographer

It will be generally admitted that Beethoven's *Fifth Symphony* is the most sublime noise that has ever penetrated the ear of man.
> – E.M. Forster (1879-1970),
> English novelist, poet,
> *Howards End* (1910)

The English may not like music, but they absolutely love the noise it makes.
> – Sir Thomas Beecham (1879-1961),
> English conductor

NONSENSE

Nothing is capable of being well set to music that is not nonsense.
> – Joseph Addison (1672-1719),
> British essayist, writer,
> in *The Spectator*

NORMAL

The trouble with normal is it always gets worse.
> – Bruce Cockburn (b.1945),
> Canadian singer-songwriter, poet,
> song lyric, *The Trouble With Normal* (1981)

NOTES

The notes I handle no better many pianists. But the pauses between the notes — ah, that is where the music resides.
> – Artur Schnabel (1882-1951),
> Austrian pianist, writer, composer,
> quoted in the *Chicago Daily News*
> (June 1958)

NOTHING

I have nothing to say and I am saying it — and that is poetry.
> – John Cage (1912-92),
> American experimental musician, composer,
> *Silence: Lecture on Nothing* (1961)

OARS

Faintly as tolls the evening chime,
Our voices keep tune and our oars keep time.
— Thomas Moore (1779-1852),
Irish poet, writer,
A Canadian Boat-Song

OPERA

Bed is the poor man's opera.

— Italian proverb

Tamino! Tamino! Ravens 16, Raiders 3!
— Jochen Schmeckenbecher,
German baritone, as Papageno, updating the
audience to a crucial football score in a San Francisco
Opera production of Mozart's *Magic Flute*,
quoted in the *San Jose Mercury* (Jan, 2001)

I do not mind what language an opera is sung in so long as
it is a language I don't understand.
— Edward Appleton (1892-1965),
English physicist, writer

An opera begins long before the curtain goes up and ends
long after it has come down. It starts in my imagination, it
becomes my life, and it stays part of my life long after I've
left the opera house.
— Maria Callas (1923-77),
American opera singer, performer

No good opera plot can be sensible, for people do not sing
when they are feeling sensible.
— W.H. Auden (1907-73),
English poet

Opera in English is, in the main, just about as sensible as baseball in Italian.
> – H.L. Mencken (1880-1956),
> American journalist, writer, music critic

You can't judge Egypt by *Aïda.*
> – Ronald Firbank (1886-1926),
> English novelist

Do it big or stay in bed.
> – Larry Kelly (b.1921),
> American opera producer

I liked your opera. I think I will set it to music.
> – Ludwig van Beethoven (1770-1827),
> German composer,
> to Italian composer Ferdinando Paër (1771-1839),
> on Paër's opera *Leonore*

Opera's when a guy gets stabbed in the back and instead of bleeding he sings.
> – Ed Gardner (1901-1963),
> American actor, writer,
> as Archie in *Duffy's Tavern,* (1983)

Going to the Opera, like getting drunk, is a sin that carries its own punishment with it, and that a very severe one.
> – Hannah More (1745-1833),
> English writer, educator,
> in a letter to her sister

An opera, like a pillory, may be said
To nail our ears down, and expose our head.
> – Edward Young (1683-1765),
> English poet,
> *Satires*

Nobody really sings in an opera – they just make loud noises.
— Amelita Galli-Curci (1889-1963),
Italian-American operatic soprano

How wonderful opera would be if there were no singers.
— Gioacchino Rossini (1792-1868),
Italian composer (of operas)

[Opera is] an exotic and irrational entertainment.
— Samuel Johnson (1709-84),
English diarist, writer, lexicographer

[Opera is] the most rococo and degraded of all art forms.
— William Morris (1834-1896),
English designer, artist, writer, poet

I would rather sing grand opera than listen to it.
— Don Herold,
American comedian

I wholly agree with Arnold Bennett, who maintained that an opera was tolerable only when sung in a language he didn't understand.
> – James Agate (1877-1947),
> English theatre-critic, writer
> (June, 1945)

I sometimes wonder which would be nicer — an opera without an interval, or an interval without an opera.
> – Ernest Newman (1869-1959),
> English music critic, writer

People are wrong when they say the opera isn't what it used to be. It *is* what it used to be. That's what's wrong with it.
> – Sir Noel Coward (1899-1973),
> English playwright, songwriter, actor, wit
> in *Design for Living* (1933)

Like German opera, too long and too loud.
> – Evelyn Waugh (1903-66),
> English writer, journalist, critic
> describing the Battle of Crete (1941)

An unalterable and unquestioned law of the musical world required that German text of French operas sung by Swedish artists should be translated into Italian for the clearer understanding of English-speaking audiences.
> – Edith Wharton (1863-1937),
> American novelist, diarist,
> in *The Age of Innocence* (1920)

I liked the opera very much. Everything but the music.
> – Sir Benjamin Britten (1913-77)
> to W.H. Auden (who wrote the libretto), on hearing
> Igor Stravinsky's *The Rake's Progress* (1951)

The opera ... is to music what a bawdy house is to a cathedral.
– H.L. Mencken (1880-56),
American journalist, writer, music critic

Sleep is an excellent way of listening to an opera.
– James Stephens III,
American comedian

The opera is like a husband with a foreign title: expensive to support, hard to understand and therefore a supreme social challenge.
– Cleveland Armory,
American writer, journalist

The first act of the three occupied three hours, and I enjoyed that in spite of the singing.
– Mark (Samuel Langhorne Clemens) Twain, (1835-2920),
American writer, wit,
in *A Tramp Abroad* (1880)

OPIATE

Music is a beautiful opiate, if you don't take it too seriously.
– Henry Miller (1891–1980),
American writer,
With Edgar Varèse in the Gobi Desert, in
The Air-Conditioned Nightmare (1945)

OPINION

No one can have a higher opinion of him than I have, and I think he's a dirty little beast.
– W. S. Gilbert (1836-1911),
English operetta libretti

ORCHESTRA

A piece for orchestra without music.
– Maurice Ravel (1875-1937),
French composer,
describing his composition *Bolero* (1928)

OVERTURES

I tried to resist his overtures, but he plied me with symphonies, quartets, chamber music and cantatas.

— S.J. Perelman (1904-79),
American writer, wit

PAGANINI, NICCOLO

I have wept only three times in my life: the first time when my earliest opera failed, the second time when, with a boating party, a truffled turkey fell into the water, and the third time when I first heard Paganini play.

— Gioacchino Rossini (1792-1868),
Italian composer

PARTON, DOLLY

I do have big tits. Always had 'em — pushed 'em up, whacked 'em around. Why not make fun of 'em? I've made a fortune with 'em.

— Dolly Parton (b.1946),
American country singer, actress

I hope people realize that there is a brain underneath the hair and a heart underneath the boobs.

— Dolly Parton (b.1946),
American country singer, actress

Storms make trees take deeper roots.

— Dolly Parton (b.1946),
American country singer, actress

I'm not offended by dumb blonde jokes because I know that I'm not dumb. I also know I'm not blonde.
– Dolly Parton (b.1946),
American country singer, actress

People make jokes about my bosoms, why don't they look underneath the breasts at the heart? It's obvious I've got big ones and if people want to assume they're not mine, then let them.
– Dolly Parton (b.1946),
American country singer, actress

You'd be surprised how much it costs to look this cheap!
– Dolly Parton (b.1946),
American country singer, actress

PASSION

What passion cannot Music raise and quell?
– John Dryden (1631-1700),
English poet, writer,
A Song for St. Cecilia's Day (1687),
set to music by G.F. Handel (1685-1758)

PEOPLE

People are stupider than anybody.
– Tom Lehrer (b.1928),
American singer-songwriter, mathematician,
on people who get offended by his songs,
in an interview with *The Onion*

There are some people that if they don't know, you can't tell them.
– Louis "Satchmo" Armstrong (1901-71),
American jazz musician, singer-songwriter, bandleader

What probably confuses people is they know a lot about me, but it quite pleases me that there's more they don't know.
— Björk Gudmundsdottir (b.1965),
Icelandic singer-songwriter, performer

Each person has inside a basic decency and goodness. If he listens to it and acts on it, he is giving a great deal of what it is the world needs most. It is not complicated but it takes courage. It takes courage for a person to listen to his own goodness and act on it.
— Pablo Casals (1876-1973),
Spanish cellist, writer

PERU

You know, wherever you go in the world, in whatever city, there is always a group of musicians from Peru playing the bloody pan pipes. Has anybody out there been to Peru? In the pedestrian zones, are there groups of musicians from Europe doing string quartets?
— Rainer Hersch,
English comedian

PHONOGRAPH

Phonograph: an irritating toy that restores life to dead noises.
— Ambrose Bierce (1842-1914),
American journalist, writer,
The Devil's Dictionary (1906)

PIANO

For me there is something ineffably new
In every new moment's arising;
and even the things I habitually do
have qualities new and surprising.

There's nothing that happens that happened before
in exactly that way in its life.
When you're playing the piano, it's rather a bore;
but it's nice when you're kissing your wife.
> – Piet Hein (1905-96),
> Danish poet, scientist, writer,
> *Novelty*, in *Grooks 3* (1970)

Nothing soothes me more after a long and maddening course
of pianoforte recitals than to sit and have my teeth drilled.
> – George Bernard Shaw (1856-1950),
> Irish-English playwright, music critic, wit

Piano. n. A parlor utensil for subduing the impenitent visitor.
It is operated by depressing the keys of the machine and the
spirits of the audience.
> – Ambrose Bierce (1842-1914),
> American journalist, writer,
> *The Devil's Dictionary* (1906)

I always make sure that the lid over the keyboard is open
before I start to play.
> – Artur Schnabel (1882-1951),
> Austrian pianist, composer,
> asked the secret of piano playing

They laughed when I sat down at the piano. But when I
started to play! ...
> – John R. Caples (b.1900),
> American writer,
> advertisement for a U.S. School of Music (circa 1925)

When she started to play, Steinway himself came down personally and rubbed his name off the piano.

– Bob (Leslie Townes) Hope (b.1903),
English-American comedian, actor, TV performer, wit,
on American comedian Phyllis Diller (b.1917)

It is said about [Henry] Cowell that he has invented tonal groups that can be played on the piano with the aid of fists and forearms! Why so coy? With one's behind one can cover many more notes!

– Paul Zschorlich,
Deutsche Zeitung,
Berlin, (Mar, 1932)

I wish the Government would put a tax on pianos for the incompetent.

– Edith Sitwell (1887-1964),
English writer

Don't tell my mother I'm in politics — she thinks I play piano in a whorehouse.

– Anon.

PLAGIARISM

It's much too good for him. He did not know what to do with it.

– G.F. Handel (1685-1759),
German-English composer, writer,
on using material composed by his rival,
Italian Giovanni Bononcini (1670-1747)

Immature artists imitate. Mature artists steal.

– Lionel Trilling (1905-75),
American teacher, literary critic

A good composer does not imitate; he steals.

– Igor Stravinsky (1882-1971),
Russian-American composer

Remember why the good Lord made your eyes — plagiarize!

– Tom Lehrer (b.1928),
American singer-songwriter, mathematician,
in his song *Lobachevsky*

POEM

A translation is no translation, he said, unless it will give you the music of a poem along with the words of it.
– John Synge (1871-1909),
Irish writer, playwright,
The Aran Islands (1907)

POETRY

Music begins to atrophy when it departs too far from the dance [and] poetry begins to atrophy when gets too far from music.
– Ezra Pound (1885-1972),
American poet, philosopher, writer,
Warning, in *ABC of Reading* (1934)

POPULAR MUSIC

There's no real lyrical content in pop music these days. It's all about ear candy and the visual tease.
– Chantal Kreviazuk (b.1974)
Canadian singer-songwriter,
quoted in *Inside Entertainment* (Dec, 2002)

Popular music is popular because a lot of people like it.
— Irving (Israel Baline) Berlin, (1888-1989),
Russian-American composer, pianist

POWER

Then cold, and hot, and moist, and dry
In order to their stations leap,
And Music's power obey.
From harmony, from heavenly harmony,
This universal frame began:
Through all the compass of the notes it ran,
The diapason closing full in Man.
— John Dryden (1631-1700),
English poet, *A Song for St. Cecilia's Day* (1687),
set to music by composer G.F. Handel (1685-1758)

PRACTISING

If I don't practice one day, I know it; two days, the critics
know it; three days, the public knows it.
— Jascha Heifetz (1901-87),
Russian-American violinist,
in the *San Francisco Examiner* (Apr, 1971)

I never practise, I always play.
— Wanda Landawska (1879-1959),
Polish concert pianist

PRAYER

Some of God's greatest gifts are unanswered prayers.
— Garth Brooks (b.1956),
American country singer-songwriter, performer

PREJUDICE

If a guy's got it, let him give it. I'm selling music, not prejudice.
> – Benny Goodman (1909-86),
> American jazz musician, bandleader,
> one of the first to form a racially mixed band

PRESLEY, ELVIS

I don't know anything about music. In my line you don't have to.
> – Elvis Presley (1935-77),
> American singer, performer, actor

Elvis was the only man from Northeast Mississippi who could shake his hips and still be loved by rednecks, cops and hippies.
> – Jimmy Buffett (b.1946)
> American singer-songwriter

Elvis is Dead, And I Don't Feel So Good Myself
> – book title by Lewis Grizzard (1947-99),
> American humorist

PRINCE OF WALES

In London, I sang in front of the Prince of Wales.
> – Georgetta Psaros,
> mezzo-soprano, formerly at Covent Garden,
> (a joke referring to any of several London pubs
> by that name, not the actual prince himself)

PSALMS

King David and King Solomon
Led merry, merry lives,
With many, many lady friends,
And many, many wives;
But when old age crept over them –
With many, many qualms! –
King Solomon wrote the Proverbs
And King David wrote the Psalms
> – James Ball Naylor (1860-1945),
> American poet, writer,
> *King David and King Solomon*, in *Vagrant Verse* (1935)

QUINTILIAN

The perfection of art is to conceal art.
> – Marcus Fabius Quintilian (35-95 BC),
> Greek philosopher, writer

QING, AI

Often my creative life has seemed like a long tunnel, dark and damp. And sometimes I wondered whether I could live through it. But I did!
> – Ai Qing (1910-96),
> Chinese poet, writer

RAIN

The sap is the music, the stem is the flute,
And the leaves are the wings of the seraph I shape

Who dances, who springs in a gold escape,
Out of the dust and the drought of the plain,
To sing with the silver hosannas of rain.
— Roy Campbell (1901-57),
South African poet,
The Palm (1928)

RAMPART

Music my rampart, and my only one.
— Edna St. Vincent Millay (1892-1950),
American poet, writer,
On Hearing a Symphony of Beethoven (1928)

RAVEL, MAURICE

Although Ravel's official biography does not mention it, I feel sure that at the age of three he swallowed a musical snuff-box, and at nine he must have been frightened by a bear. To both phenomena he offers repeated testimony: he is constantly tinkling high on the harps and celesta, or is growling low in the bassoons and double-basses.
— Edward Robinson,
The American Mercury, New York, (May 1932)

Who can unravel Ravel?
— Louis Elson, Boston *Daily Advertiser,*
(Dec, 1913)

REALITY

Those wedded to music belong to the realm of the
constant-ephemeral — a visionary realm requiring oft-
time the painful renunciation of reality.

– Sir Yehudi Menuhin (1916-1999),
American-English, violinist, conductor, writer,
in his preface to *A Musician's Dictionary* (1990)

REAR

I could serve coffee using my rear as a ledge.

– Jennifer Lopez (b.1970),
American singer, performer, actress

REGER, MAX

Reger might be epitomized as a composer whose name is
the same either forward or backward, and whose music,
curiously, often displays the same characteristic.

– Irving Kolodin,
critic New York *Sun* (Nov. 1934)

REMEMBRANCE

The setting sun, and music at the close,
As the last taste of sweets, is sweetest last,
Writ in remembrance more than things long past.

– William Shakespeare (1564-1616),
English poet, playwright,
John of Gaunt, in *Richard II*, act 2, scene 1, lines 12-14

REPERTOIRE

I do not see any good reason why the devil should have all the good tunes.

> – Rowland Hill (1744-1833),
> English clergyman, writer

I know only two tunes: one of them is *Yankee Doodle* and the other one isn't.

> – Ulysses S. Grant (1822-85),
> American Civil War
> general, 18th U.S. president

REPETITION

Today, music heralds ... the establishment of a society of repetition in which nothing will happen anymore.

> – Jacques Attali (b.1943),
> Algerian-French economist, writer,
> *Noise: The Political Economy of Music* (1977)

RESPONSIBILITY

It'd be stupid for me to sit here and say that there aren't kids who took up to me, but my responsibility is not to them. I'm not a babysitter.

> – "Eminem" Marshall Mathers (b.1972),
> American rapper-songwriter, performer

REST

There's no music in a "rest," Katie, that I know of: but there's the making of music in it. And people are always missing that part of the life-melody.

– John Ruskin (1819-1900),
English art critic, essayist, writer,
Ethics of the Dust, Lecture 4: The Crystal Orders (1866)

– the rest is silence.

– William Shakespeare (1564-1616),
English poet, playwright,
Hamlet, in *Hamlet*, act 5, scene 2, line 358

RETIREMENT

Musicians don't retire; they stop when there's no more music in them.

– Louis "Satchmo" Armstrong (1901-71),
American jazz trumpeter, singer-songwriter, bandleader

RIMSKY-KORSAKOV, NIKOLAI

Rimsky-Korsakov — what a name! It suggests fierce whiskers stained with vodka!

– *Musical Courier*,
New York (Oct, 1897)

ROCK AND ROLL

Rock appeals to the intelligence without interference from the intellect.
— Chester Anderson (1932-91),
American journalist, writer

Most people get into bands for three very simple rock and roll reasons: to get laid, to get fame, and to get rich.
— Bob Geldof (b.1954),
Irish musician, singer-songwriter, (Boomtown Rats)
quoted in *Melody Maker* (Aug, 1977)

It's Only Rock 'n Roll
— Rolling Stones album title

Boy George is all England needs — another queen who can't dress.
— Joan Rivers (b.1933),
American comedian, TV commentator

It's one thing to want to save lives in Ethiopia, but it's another thing to inflict so much torture on the British public.
— Morrissey (Stephen Patrick Morrissey) 1959),
on Bob Geldof's fundraiser for Band Aid (1984)

If white bread could sing, it would sound like Olivia Newton-John.
— Anon.

The popular music industry has tried, repeatedly, to do with music what Ford attempts with cars. It works better with cars.

> – Tony Palmer, (b.1941)
> English writer, musician, TV producer,
> *All You Need is Love: The Story of Popular Music* (1976)

I've always said that pop music is disposable. ... If it wasn't disposable, it'd be a pain in the fuckin' arse.

> – Sir Elton (Reginald Kenneth Dwight) John (b.1947),
> English singer-songwriter, composer, pianist

They look like boys whom any self-respecting mum would lock in the bathroom.

> – The London *Daily Express*,
> on The Rolling Stones (1964)

When I first started playing guitar, you didn't play gigs so much as just went out and tested your gear.

> – Jeff Beck (b.1944),
> English musician, singer-songwriter (The Yardbirds)

If Patty Hearst were on United Artists Records, she never would have been found.

> – Dean Torrence (b.1940),
> American musician duo (Jan & Dean)

The image we have would be hard for Mickey Mouse to maintain.

> – Karen Carpenter (1950-83),
> American singer-songwriter, drummer,
> (The Carpenters)

We're Pat Boone, only cleaner.

> – Richard Carpenter (b.1946),
> American singer-songwriter, pianist,
> (The Carpenters)

My persona is so confused it even confuses me.
> – David Bowie (David Robert Jones) (b.1947),
> English singer-songwriter, actor

People take us far too seriously. We're going to have to start being far more stupid.
> – David Byrne (b.1952),
> Scottish-American singer-songwriter,
> (Talking Heads)

I don't think anybody ever made it with a girl because they had a Tom Waits album on their shelves. I've got all three, and it never helped me.
> – Tom Waits (b.1949),
> American singer-songwriter

Reporting I'm drunk is like saying there was a Tuesday last week.
> – Grace (Grace Barnett Wing) Slick (b.1939),
> American singer-songwriter, performer
> (Jefferson Airplane, later Jefferson Starship)

I don't expect *Short People* to be a big commercial success in Japan.
> – Randy Newman (b.1943),
> American singer-songwriter, pianist, film composer

We wanted to see America. It wasn't entirely successful. I kept falling asleep. It was a long drive.
> – Mick Jones (b.1955),
> English musician, singer-songwriter (The Clash)

I'm going to run for President and when I get elected I'll assassinate myself. That'll set a precedent.
> – Spencer Dryden (b.1938),
> American musician (Jefferson Airplane,
> later Jefferson Starship)

I manage to look so young because I'm mentally retarded.
— Deborah Harry (b.1945),
American singer-songwriter, performer (Blondie)

We would rather be rich than famous. That is, more rich and slightly less famous.
— John Lennon (1940-80),
English musician, singer-songwriter, actor
(The Beatles)

I'm the man who put the unk into the funk.
— Muddy (McKinley Morganfield) Waters, 1915-83),
American blues musician, singer-songwriter

I'm a rompin', stompin', piano-playing son of a bitch. A mean son of a bitch. But a great son of a bitch.
— Jerry Lee Lewis (b.1935),
American singer-songwriter, pianist, performer,
Time magazine, (March 1983)

I never considered myself the greatest, but I am the best.
— Jerry Lee Lewis (b.1935),
American singer-songwriter, pianist, performer

The Rolling Stones are like a dinosaur attached to an iron lung.

— Tom Robinson (b.1950),
English singer-songwriter

In America, Debbie Harry is the girl next door only if you live in a bad neighborhood.

— Roy Carr, (b.1939)
English journalist, writer, musician,
New Musical Express

ROSE

Red Rose, proud Rose, sad Rose of all my days!
Come near me, while I sing the ancient ways!

— William Butler Yeats (1865-1939),
Irish poet, playwright,
To the Rose Upon the Rood of Time (1895)

ROSSINI, GIOACCHINO

Rossini would have been a great composer if his teacher had spanked him enough on his backside.

— Ludwig van Beethoven (1770-1827),
German composer

Dear God — here it is, finished, this poor little Mass. ... Little science, some heart, that's all there is to it. Be blessed, then, and grant me a place in Paradise.

— Gioacchino Rossini (1792-1868),
Italian composer, in an inscription
at the end of his *Petite Messe Solennelle* (1863)

RHYTHM

Music above all, and for this
Prefer an uneven rhythm

> — Paul Verlaine (1844-96),
> French poet, writer,
> *Jadis et Naguère, L'Art Poetique* (1884)

ROYALTIES

And the royalites went to Royalty

> — Michael Flanders (1922-75),
> English singer-comedic lyricist, pianist, writer,
> on *Greensleeves* having been written
> by Henry VIII,
> (*At the Drop of a Hat*)

SATIRE

You can't be satirical and not be offensive to somebody.

> — Tom Lehrer (b.1928),
> American singer-songwriter, mathematician,
> in an interview with *The Onion*

SAY

Say It With Music

> — Irving (Israel Baline) Berlin (1888-1989),
> Russian-American composer, pianist,
> song title

SAXOPHONE

The saxophone is the embodied spirit of beer.
– Arnold Bennett (attrib.)

Don't play the saxophone. Let it play you.
– Charlie "Bird" Christopher Parker Jr. (1920–1955),
American jazz musician, composer

SCHOENBERG, ARNOLD

[Schoenberg's *Violin Concerto*] combines the best sound effects of a hen yard at feeding time, a brisk morning in Chinatown and practice hour at a busy music conservatory. The effect on the vast majority of hearers is that of a lecture on the fourth dimension delivered in Chinese.
– Edwin H. Schloss,
Philadelphia *Record* (Dec, 1940)

SCRIABIN, ALEXANDER

The voluptuous dentist.
– Aldous Huxley (1894-1963),
English writer, essayist,
on Russian composer Alexander Scriabin (1872-1915)

SHAW, GEORGE BERNARD

Bernard Shaw has no enemies, but is intensely disliked by his friends.
– Oscar Wilde (1854-1900),
Irish-English playwright, novelist, wit

The way Bernard Shaw believes in himself is very refreshing in these atheistic days when so many believe in no God at all.

> – Israel Zangwill (1864-1926),
> English writer, political activist

SILENCE

After silence, that which comes nearest to expressing the inexpressible is music.

> – Aldous Huxley (1894-1963),
> English writer, essayist,
> *Music at Night* (1931)

Silence is more musical than any song.

> – Christina Rossetti (1830-94),
> English poet

Elected Silence, sing to me
And beat upon my whorlèd ear,
Pipe me to pastures still and be
The music that I care to hear

> – Gerard Manley Hopkins (1844-89),
> English poet,
> *The Habit of Perfection* (1918)

The silent man is the best to listen to.

> – Japanese proverb

No voice; but oh! the silence sank
Like music on my heart.

> – Samuel Taylor Coleridge (1772-1834),
> English poet,
> *The Rime of the Ancient Mariner* (1798)

I believe in the discipline of silence and could talk for hours about it.

> – George Bernard Shaw (1856-1950),
> Irish-English playwright, music critic, wit

SINATRA, FRANK

I wish Frank Sinatra would just shut up and sing.

> – Lauren (Betty Joan Perske) Bacall (b.1924),
> American film actress

Sinatra's idea of Paradise is a place where there are plenty of women and no newspapermen. He doesn't know it, but he'd be better off if it were the other way round.

> – Humphry Bogart (1899-1957),
> American film actor

I didn't want to find a horse's head in my bed.

> – Paul Anka (b.1941),
> Canadian-American singer-songwriter,
> on why he gave *My Way* to Frank Sinatra

SINGERS AND SINGING

I cannot switch my voice. My voice is not like an elevator going up and down.

> – Maria Callas (1923-77),
> American opera singer, performer

Being a singer is a natural gift. It means I'm using to the highest degree possible the gift that God gave me to use. I'm happy with that.

> – Aretha Franklin (b.1942),
> American R&B singer, performer

Regard your voice as capital in the bank. Sing on your
interest and your voice will last.
                                        — Lauritz Melchior (1890-1973),
                                                Danish operatic tenor

It's hardly the freshest approach to music. I mean, other
people sing. I'm not the first person to yodel.
                                        — Ashley MacIsaac (b.1974),
                                        Canadian musician, fiddler,
                                        on his turn as vocalist,
                        quoted in the *National Post* (April 2003)

I can't sing. As a singist I am not a success. I am saddest
when I sing. So are those who hear me. They are sadder
even than I am.
                                — Artemus (Charles Farrar Browne) Ward (1834-67),
                                        American journalist, humorist

ll singers have this fault: if asked to sing among friends they are never so inclined; if unasked, they never leave off.

> – Horace (65-8 B.C)
> (Quintus Horatius Flaccus, Italian poet), *Satires*

Reasons briefly set down by the author to persuade every one to learn to sing:

First, it is a knowledge easily taught, and quickly learned, where there is a good Master and an apt scholar.

2. The exercise of singing is delightful to Nature, and good to preserve the health of Man.

3. It doth strengthen all parts of the brest and doth open the pipes.

7. There is not any Music of Instruments whatsoever, comparable to that which is made of the voices of Man, where the voices are good, and the same well sorted and ordered.

8. The better the voice is, the meeter it is to honour and serve God therewith: and the voice of Man is chiefly to be employed to that end.

Since singing is so good a thing,
I wish all men would learn to sing.

> – William Byrd (1543-1623),
> English composer, writer,
> in the preface to *Psalmes, Sonets, & Songs* (1588)

I hear America singing, the varied carols I hear.

> – Walt Whitman (1819-92),
> American poet, writer,
> *Leaves of Grass: I Hear America Singing* (1855-92)

The only thing better than singing is more singing.

> – Ella Fitzgerald (1918-96),
> American jazz singer, performer

I'm a musician at heart, I know I'm not really a singer. I couldn't compete with real singers. But I sing because the public buys it.
> – Nat "King" (Nathaniel Adams Coles) Cole (1919-65),
> American singer-songwriter, pianist

Swans sing before they die — 'twere no bad thing
> – Samuel Taylor Coleridge (1772-1834),
> English poet, writer,
> *Epigram on a Volunteer Singer*

Ya know whatta you do when you shit?
Singing, it's the same thing, only up!
> – Enrico Caruso (1873-1921),
> Italian-American opera singer

Anything that is too stupid to be spoken is sung.
> – Voltaire (Francois Marie Arouet 1694-1778),
> French philosopher, writer

Sometimes my voice can make *me* cry.
> – Leonard Cohen (b.1934),
> Canadian poet-songwriter,
> quoted by Christopher Jones,
> *Now* magazine (Nov, 1988)

Leonard Cohen gives you the feeling that your dog just died.
> – *Q* magazine

You sang like a composer.
> – Jules Massanet (1842-1912),
> French composer,
> to a tenor whose singing he disliked

A vile beastly rottonheaded foolbegotten brazenthroated pernicious piggish screaming, tearing, roaring, perplexing, spitmecrackle crashmecringle insane ass of a woman is practising howling below-stairs with a brute of a singingmaster so horribly, that my head is nearly off.
— Edward Lear (1812-88),
English nonsense writer,
in a letter to Lady Strachey (Jan. 1859)

A base barreltone voice.
— James Joyce (1882-1941),
Irish writer, poet,
in *Ulysses* (1922).

I am saddest when I sing; so are those that hear me; they are sadder ever than I am.
— Artemus (Charles Farrar Browne) Ward (1834-67),
American journalist, wit

My mother used to say that my elder sister has a beautiful contralto voice. This was arrived at not through her ability to reach the low notes — which she could not do — but because she could not reach the high ones.
— Samuel Butler (1834-1902),
English writer, essayist,
Note-Books

She was a singer who had to take any note above A with her eyebrows.
— Montague Glass (1877-1934)
English-American humorist, playright

She was a town-and-country soprano of the kind often used for augmenting grief at a funeral.
— George Ade (1866-1944)
American dramatist, wit

The higher the voice the smaller the intellect.
— Ernest Newman (1869-1959),
English writer, music critic, (attrib.)

I can hold a note as long as the Chase National Bank.
— Ethel Merman (1908-84),
American singer, actress

Her voice sounded like an eagle being goosed.
— Ralph Novak on Yoko Ono (b.1933),
People magazine (Dec. 1985)

We've had a request from the audience. But we're going to keep singing anyway.

— Anon.

SIRENS

Blest pair of Sirens, pledges of Heaven's joy,
Sphere-born harmonious sisters, Voice and Verse,
Wed your divine sounds, and mixt power employ,
Dead things with inbreathed sense able to pierce;
And to our high-raised phantasy present
That undisturbed song of pure consent,
Aye sung before the sapphire-coloured throne
To him that sits thereon,
With saintly shout and solemn jubilee.
— John Milton (1608-74),
English poet, writer,
At a Solemn Musick (1634)

SIXPENCE

Sing a song of sixpence,
A pocket full of rye,
Four and twenty blackbirds
Baked in a pie;
When the pie was opened
The birds began to sing;
Wasn't that a dainty dish
To set before a king?

> – *Sing a Song of Sixpence*,
> English nursery rhyme,(16th century)

SLEEP

Music, ho, music such as charmeth sleep!

> – William Shakespeare (1564-1616),
> English poet, playwright,
> Titania, in *A Midsummer Night's Dream*,
> act 4, scene 1, line 83

SONG(S)

It is the best of all trades, to make songs, and the second best to sing them.

> – Hillaire Belloc (1870-1953),
> French-English poet, writer, politician,
> *On Song*, in *On Everything* (1909)

How shall we sing the Lord's song in a strange land?

> – *Psalms* 137:4

The popular song is America's greatest ambassador.

> – Sammy Cahn (1913-93),
> American composer, pianist

You can cage the singer, but not the song.

– Harry Belafonte (b.1927),
American singer, actor, activist

A song without music is a lot like H2 without the O.

– Ira (Israel) Gershwin (1896-1983),
American composer, lyricist, pianist

I hand him a lyric and get out of his way.

– Oscar Hammerstein II (1895-1960)
American composer, lyricist,
on composer Richard Rodgers (1902-80)

I would much rather have written the best song of a nation than its noblest epic.

– Edgar Allan Poe (1809-49),
American writer, poet

There's not really an emotion I put in a song that I haven't had. I've been lonesome. I've been rejected. I've been bad. I've been drunk... I know the mistakes I've made the wrongs that have been done to me – and I have a real good memory.

–Harlan Howard (1927-2002),
American singer-songwriter,
quoted in *The Daily Telegraph* (March 2002)

Unless I'm wrong
I but obey
The urge of a song:
I'm – bound – away!

– Robert Frost (1874-1963),
American poet, writer
Away! (1962)

I made my song a coat
Covered with embroideries

Out of old mythologies
From heel to throat;
But the fools caught it,
Wore it in the world's eye
As though they'd wrought it.
Song, let them take it
For there's more enterprise
In walking naked.

> – William Butler Yeats (1865-1939),
> Irish poet, playwright,
> *A Coat* (1914)

The Aim was Song.

> – Robert Frost (1874-1963),
> American poet,
> poem title *New Hampshire*, (1923)

I have wished a bird would fly away,
And not sing by my house all day;
Have clapped my hands at him from the door
When it seemed as if I could bear no more.
The fault must partly have been in me.
The bird was not to blame for is key.
And of course there must be something wrong
In wanting to silence any song.

> – Robert Frost (1874-1963),
> American poet,
> *A Minor Bird*

I'm nothing special, in fact I'm a bit of a bore,
If I tell a joke, you've probably heard it before,
But I have a talent, a wonderful thing,
'Cause everyone listens when I start to sing,
I'm so grateful and proud,
All I want is to sing it out loud.

So I say,
Thank you for the music, the songs I'm singing,
Thanks for all the joy they're bringing,
Who can live without it, I ask in all honesty,
What would life be?
Without a song or a dance what are we?

So I say thank you for the music,
For giving it to me.
                    — Benny Anderson, Bjorn Ulvaeus,
            Swedish musicians, singer-songwriters (ABBA),
                        Thank You for the Music (1977)

Song: the licenced medium for bawling in public things too silly or sacred to be uttered in ordinary speech.
— Oliver Herford (1863-1935), American writer, artist

There was an Old Person of Tring
Who, when somebody asked her sing,
Replied, "Aren't it odd?
I never tell *God Save the Weasel* from *Pop Goes the King*."
— Anon., in *The New York Times Magazine* (1946)

Once in every lifetime a really beautiful song comes along. ... Until it does, I'd like to do this one.
                    — Sir Cliff (Harry Webb) Richard, (b.1940),
                                in his stage act (1983)

SONG TITLES

How Can I Miss You If You Won't Go Away?
— song title *Soul*

Blue Turning Grey Over You
— barbershop song title

If Today Was a Fish, I'd Throw It Back In
— song title

I'm So Miserable Without You
It's Almost Like Having You Here
— song title by Stephen Bishop

Drop Kick Me, Jesus, Through the Goal Posts of Life
— song title

She Got the Gold Mine,
I Got the Shaft
— song title by Jerry Reed

When My Love Comes Back from the Ladies' Room
Will I Be Too Old to Care?
— song title by Lewis Grizzard (1947-99),
American humorist

Let knowledge grow from more to more,
But more of reverence within us dwell;
That mind and soul, according well,
May make one music as before.
— Alfred Lord Tennyson (1809-92),
English poet,
In Memoriam (1850)

I will not say "God rest his soul," for he had none.
— George Bernard Shaw (1856-1950),
Irish-English playwright, music critic, wit,
on the death of Italian opera composer
Gioacchino Rossini (1792-1868)

SOUND(S)

I don't care much about music. What I like is sounds.
— Dizzy Gillespie (b.1917),
American jazz musician, composer, bandleader

Music proposes. Sound disposes.
— Babette Deutsch (1895-1982),
American poet,
Electronic Concert, line 1 (1969)
a parody of "Man proposes; God disposes,"
Thomas à Kempis (1380-1471), *Imatio Christi* (ca. 1420)

Not many sounds in life, and I include all urban and all
rural sounds, exceed in interest a knock at the door.
— Charles Lamb (1775-1834), English essayist, writer
Essays of Elia: Valentine's Day (1823)

The plain fact is that music per se means nothing; it is
sheer sound, and the interpreter can do no more with it
than his own capacities, mental and spiritual, will allow,
and the same applies to the listener.
— Sir Thomas Beecham (1879-1961),
English conductor,
in *Mingled Chime* (1944)

SOUR

How sour sweet music is
When time is broke and no proportion kept!
So it is in the music of men's lives.
> – William Shakespeare (1564-1616),
> English poet, playwright, Richard,
> in *Richard II*, act 5, scene 5, line 42

SPEECH

The music that can deepest reach,
And cure all ill, is cordial speech.
> – Ralph Waldo Emerson (1803-82),
> American philosopher, writer,
> *May-Day and Other Pieces: Merlin's Song*

SPHERE(S)

… music from the spheres.
> – William Shakespeare (1564-1616),
> English poet, playwright,
> Olivia, in *Twelfth Night*, act 3, scene 1, line 109

This *must* be music, said he, of the *spears*,
For I am cursed if each note of it doesn't run
through one!
> – Thomas Moore (1779-1852),
> Irish poet, writer

O Music, sphere-descended maid,
Friend of Pleasure, Wisdom's aid!
> William Collins (1721-1759),
> English poet,
> *The Passions* (1747)

The music of the spheres! ...
Most heavenly music!
It nips me unto list'ning, and thick slumber
Hangs upon mine eyes.

> – William Shakespeare (1564-1616),
> English poet, playwright,
> Pericles, in *Pericles*, act 5, scene 1, lines 229-35

Sure there is music even in the beauty, and the silent note which Cupid strikes, far sweeter than the sound of an instrument. For there is music wherever there is a harmony, order, proportion; and thus far we may maintain the music of the spheres.

> – Sir Thomas Browne (1605-1682),
> English scientist, philospher,
> *Religio Medici* (1642)

SPIRIT

Dust as we are, the immortal spirit grows
Like harmony in music; there is a dark
Inscrutable workmanship that reconciles
Discordant elements, makes them cling together
In one society.

> – William Wordsworth (1770-1850),
> English poet,
> *The Prelude*

Just as my fingers on these keys
Make music, so the self-same sounds
On my spirit make a music, too.

> – Wallace Stevens (1879-1955),
> American poet, writer,
> *Peter Quince at the Clavier* (1923)

STARDOM

I'm an instant star. Just add water and stir.
– David (David Robert Jones) Bowie (b.1947),
English singer-songwriter, actor

STRAVINSKY, IGOR

Stravinsky's *Symphony for Wind Instruments* written in memory of Debussy ... was greeted with cheers, hisses, and laughter. I had no idea Stravinsky disliked Debussy so much as this. If my own memories of a friend were as painful as Stravinsky's of Debussy seem to be, I would try to forget him.
– Ernest Newman (1868-1959),
English music critic, writer,
Musical Times, London (July 1921)

[Stravinsky's music is] Bach on the wrong notes.
– Sergei Prokofiev (1891-1953),
Russian composer

The Rite of Spring

Who wrote this fiendish *Rite of Spring*,
What right had he to write the thing,
Against our helpless ears to fling
Its crash, clash, cling, clang, bing, bang, bing?

And then to call it *Rite of Spring*,
The season when on joyous wing
The birds melodious carols sing
And harmony's in everything!

He who could write the *Rite of Spring*,
If I be right, by right should swing!
– Boston *Herald* (Feb. 1924)

The most invigorating sound I heard was a restive neighbor winding his watch.
– Mildred Norton,
on a concert of Igor Stravinsky,
Los Angeles *Daily News* (Nov, 1952)

STRING QUARTETS

Most string quartets have a basement and an attic, and the lift is not working.
– Neville Cardus (1889-1975),
English journalist, writer,
The Delights of Music (1966)

STUDY

We must believe in luck, for how else can we explain the success of those we don't like?
– Jean Cocteau (1889-1963),
French film director, dramatist, poet, writer

I must study politics and war, that my sons my have liberty to study mathematics and philosophy, geography, natural history and naval architecture, in order to give their children a right to study painting, poetry, music, architecture, statuary, tapestry, and porcelain.
– John Adams (1735-1826),
American Statesman, president after
George Washington, 1797-1808), in a
letter to his wife, Abigail, 1780 (pub. 1841)

STYLE

Frequently composers try to reproduce the musical sound of a specific age or locale, often with some success, but I think it's a mistake. It leaves the writer wide open to comparison — usually unfavorable — with the real thing, and at best reveals only re-creative, rather than creative, skills.

> – Richard Rodgers (1902-80),
> American composer, pianist,
> in *Musical Stages: An Autobiography* (1975)

SUCCESS

The toughest thing about success is that you've got to keep on being a success.

> – Irving (Israel Baline) Berlin, (1888-1989),
> Russian-American composer, pianist

SUICIDE

I tried to commit suicide one day. It was a very Woody Allen-type suicide. I turned on the gas and left all the windows open.
> – Sir Elton (Reginald Kenneth Dwight) John (b.1947),
> English singer-songwriter, composer, pianist

Anybody who has listened to certain kinds of music, or read certain kinds of poetry, or heard certain kinds of performances on the concertina, will admit that even suicide has its brighter aspects.
> – Stephen Leacock (1869-1944),
> Canadian humorist, writer

SWAN

The silver swan, who living hath no note,
When death approached unlocked her silent throat;
Leaning her breast against the reedy shore,
Thus sang her first and last, and sung no more;
Farewell, all joys; O death, come close mine eyes;
More geese than swans now live, more fools than wise.
> – Orlando Gibbons (1583-1625),
> English composer,
> *The First Set of Madrigals and Motets* (1612)

The jalous swan, ayens his deth that singeth.
> – Geoffrey Chaucer (ca.1343-1400),
> English poet, writer,
> *The Parliament of Fowls* (1380-86)

I will play the swan and die in music
> – William Shakespeare (1564-1616),
> English poet, playwright,
> Emelia, in *Othello*, act 5, scene 2, line 245

Let music sound while he doth make his choice;
Then if he lose he makes a swan-like end,
Fading in music.
— William Shakespeare (1564-1616),
English poet, playwright,
Portia, in *The Merchant of Venice*, act 3, scene 2, line 43

STYLE

I've gotten sick of trying. It's not country. But I love country music. It's not jazz. But I love jazz. It's not really pop music. It's not soul. It's not blues. But everyone that played on the record is influenced by all that stuff. So, it's just a collection of songs. Some are originals. Some you've heard before. They're just songs.
— Norah Jones (b.1979),
American singer-songwriter,
asked to describethe style of her hit debut album,
Come Away With Me, quoted in *Inside Entertainment*
(July 2003)

TALENT

I believe that since my life began
The most I've had is just
A talent to amuse.
> – Sir Noel Coward (1899-1973),
> English playwright, singer-songwriter, actor, wit,
> song *If Love Were All* (1929)

TASTE

She was one of the people who say I don't know anything about music really, but I know what I like.
> – Max Beerbohm (1872-1956),
> English writer, journalist,
> *Zuleika Dobson* (1911)

TCHAIKOVSKY, PETER ILLYCH

One special pleasure I derived in composing the score for *Chee-Chee* was a musical joke that I used toward the end of the second act. As the son of the Grand Eunuch was being led off for his emasculation operation, he was accompanied by a triumphal march, in the middle of which I inserted several bars of Tchaikovsky's *Nutcracker Suite*. I found it gratifying that at almost every performance there were two or three individuals with ears musically sharp enough to appreciate the joke.
> – Richard Rodgers (1902-80),
> American composer, pianist,
> in *Musical Stages: An Autobiography* (1975)

Tchaikovsky's love life was, to put it bluntly, confused.
— David W. Barber (b.1958),
Canadian journalist, humorist and musician,
Bach, Beethoven and the Boys (1986)

Tchaikovsky's *First Piano Concerto*, like the first pancake, is a flop.
— Nicolai Soloviev,
Novoye Vremya, St. Petersburg (Nov, 1875)

Friedrich Vischer once observed, speaking of obscene pictures, that they stink to the eye. Tchaikovsky's *Violin Concerto* gives us for the first time the hideous notion that there can be music that stinks to the ear.
— Eduard Hanslick (1825-1904),
Austrian music critic, writer,
Neue Freie Presse, Vienna (Dec. 1881)

TEACHER

The music teacher came twice each week to bridge the awful gap between Dorothy and Chopin.
— George Ade (1866-1944),
American dramatist, writer, wit (attrib.)

TENORS

Tenors get women by the score.
— James Joyce (1882-1941),
Irish writer, poet,
in *Ulysses* (1922)

The cast of *Boris Godunov* includes one character called 'An Idiot.' The role is of course sung by a tenor.
> – David W. Barber (b.1958),
> Canadian journalist, humorist, musician,
> *When the Fat Lady Sings* (1990)

THEATRE

The theatre is not the place for the musician. When the curtain is up the music interrupts the actor, and when it is down, the music interrupts the audience.
> – Sir Arthur Sullivan (1842-1900),
> English composer

TONALITY

At university, we were taught to avoid the obvious, and very much reprimanded if we used any kind of tonality. Music was atonal, arhythmic, amelodic, a-everything. It wasn't communicating to a larger public.
> – Marjan Mozetich (b.1948),
> Canadian composer,
> quoted in *Words & Music* (Summer 2003)

TOUGH

I used to dress in black every day and pretend to be tough.
> – Deborah Harry (b.1945),
> American singer-songwriter, performer (Blondie),
> on her teen years in New Jersey

TREASON(S)

The man that hath not music in himself,
Nor is not moved with concord of sweet sounds,
Is fit for treasons, stratagems and spoils;
The motions of his spirit are dull as night,
And his affections dark as Erebus:
Let no such man be trusted.
> – William Shakespeare (1564-1616),
> English poet, playwright, Lorenzo,
> in *The Merchant of Venice*, act 5, scene 1, lines 83-88

TRUMPET(S)

Blow up the trumpet in the new moon
> – *Psalms*, 81:3

The trumpet shall sound, and the dead shall be raised incorruptible, and we shall be changed.
> – *I Corinthians*, 15:52

The trumpet's loud clangor
Excites us to arms.
> – John Dryden (1631-1700),
> English poet, writer,
> *A Song for St. Cecilia's Day* (1687),
> set to music by G.F. Handel (1685-1758)

The trumpet shall be heard on high
The dead shall live, the living die,
And Music shall untune the sky!
> – John Dryden (1631-1700),
> English poet, writer,
> *A Song for St. Cecilia's Day* (1687),
> set to music by G.F. Handel (1685-1758)

Where the bright Seraphim, in burning row,
Their loud uplifted angel-trumpets blow;
And the Cherubic host, in thousand quires,
Touch their immortal harps of golden wires,
With those just Spirits that wear victorious palms.
Hymns devout and holy psalms
Singing everlastingly.

> – John Milton (1608-74),
> English poet,
> *At a Solemn Musick* (1634)

The silver, snarling trumpets' gan to chide.

> – John Keats (1795-1821),
> English poet,
> *Poems: The Eve of St. Agnes* (1820)

Sound the trumpet till around
You make the listening shores rebound.
On the sprightly oboy play.
All the instruments of joy
That skilful numbers can employ
To celebrate the glory of this day

> – Anon., text from *Come, Ye Sons of Art*,
> a birthday ode for Queen Mary (1694), set to music by
> Henry Purcell (1659-95)
> English composer

TRUTH

You can't cheat in mathematics or poetry or music, because
they're based on truth.

> – John Steinbeck (1902-68),
> American novelist, writer,
> *Sweet Thursday* (1954)

Truth is like the sun. You can shut it out for a time, but it ain't goin' away.

> – Elvis Presley (1935-77),
> American singer, performer, actor

TUNING

Gentleman, take your pick!

> – Sir Thomas Beecham (1879-1961),
> English conductor,
> on hearing an oboist giving an A for tuning.

TURTLE

The flowers appear on the earth; the time of the singing of birds is come, and the voice of the turtle is heard in our land.

> – *Song of Solomon*, 2:12

UKULELE

Unless accompanied by the Ukulele, the native [Hawaiian] Hula and Luau dances would be like meat without salt.

> – N.B. Bailey,
> American music educator,
> *A Practical Method for Self-Instruction
> on the Ukulele and Banjo Ukulele* (1914)

UPDIKE, JOHN

... Nor was God in the churches, save rarely, as when a bass organ note left pedalled from the Amen rattled the leadings of the apostles' stained-glass halos and echoed from the darkest, not-even-at-Easter-inhabited rear of the balcony like a waking animal groaning from his burrow.
– John Updike (b.1932),
American writer, essayist,
A Month of Sundays (1974)

Girls in their first blush of adolescence, carrying fawn-colored flute cases and pallid folders of music, shuffle by me; their awkwardness is lovely, like the stance of a bather testing the sea.
– John Updike (b.1932),
American writer, essayist,
The Music School (1966)

From all directions sounds – of pianos, oboes, clarinets – arrive like hints of another world, a world where angels fumble, pause, and begin again.
– John Updike (b.1932),
American writer, essayist,
The Music School (1966)

Listening, I remember what learning music is like, how impossibly difficult and complex seem the first fingerings, the first decipherings of that unique language which freights each note with a double meaning of position and duration, a language as finicking as Latin, as laconic as Hebrew, as surprising to the eye as Persian or Chinese. How mysterious appears that calligraphy of parallel spaces, swirling clefs, superscribed ties, superscribed decrescendos, dots and sharps and flats! How great looms the gap between the first gropings of vision and the first stammerings of percussion! Vision, timidly, becomes percussion, percussion becomes music, music becomes emotion, emotion becomes – vision. Few of us have the heart to follow this circle to its end.

> – John Updike (b.1932),
> American writer, essayist,
> *The Music School* (1966)

USTINOV, SIR PETER

I was irrevocably betrothed to laughter, the sound of which has always seemed to me the most civilized music in the world.

> – Sir Peter Ustinov (b.1921),
> English writer, actor, wit,
> *Dear Me* (1977), ch. 3

WILLIAMS, RALPH VAUGHAN

Listening to the *Fifth Symphony* of Ralph Vaughan Williams is like staring at a cow for 45 minutes.

> – Aaron Copland (1900-90),
> American composer

I don't know whether I like it, but it's what I meant.

> – Ralph Vaughan Williams (1872-1958),
> English composer,
> on a passage in his *Fourth Symphony*

It looks wrong, and it sounds wrong; but it's right.

> – Ralph Vaughan Williams (1872-1958)
> English composer,
> also on a passage in his *Fourth Symphony*

Verdi, Giuseppe

Verdi was intended by nature for a composer, but I am afraid the genius given him — like girls kissing each other — is decided waste of the raw material.
> – *Dwight's Journal of Music,*
> Boston (July 1855)

Vibration(s)

Out of me unworthy and unknown
The vibrations of deathless music.
> – Edgar Lee Masters (1869-1950),
> American poet, playwright,
> *Spoon River Anthology: Anne Rutledge* (1915)

Verdi is the only eminent composer in history who was also a successful farmer.
> – Donald J. Grout (1902-87),
> American writer, music historian,
> *A History of Western Music* (1960, rev. 1973)

Music, when soft voices die,
Vibrates in the memory;
Odors, when sweet violets sicken,
Live within the sense they quicken.
> – Percy Bysshe Shelley (1792-1822),
> English poet,
> *To —: Music, When Soft Voices Die* (1821)

VIOLIN

As a child I was impelled to the violin, it seemed to respond to a desire for self expression. The violin ... is part nearly of the body, vibrates with it ... the tone is something which you make alone, it is flexible, it is something intimate ... it is something mysterious ...
> – Sir Yehudi Menuhin (1916-1999),
> American-English, violinist, conductor, writer,
> quoted in a BBC interview (1955)

Life is like playing a violin in public and learning the instrument as one goes on.
> – Samuel Butler (1835-1902),
> English writer, essayist

Violinist: a man who is always up to his chin in music.
> – Anon.

You see, our fingers are circumcised, which gives it a very good dexterity, you know, particularly the pinky.
> – Itzhak Perlman (b.1945),
> Israeli-American violinist,
> replying to a comment that so many
> great violinists are Jewish

VISION

Just because a man lacks the use of his eyes doesn't mean
he lacks vision.
> – Stevie (Steveland Judkins) Wonder (b.1950),
> American musician, singer-songwriter, pianist

VIVALDI, ANTONIO

All in all, Vivaldi composed about 450 concertos of one
sort or another. People who find his music too repetitious
are inclined to say that he wrote the same concerto 450
times. This is hardly fair: he wrote two concertos, 225
times each.
> – David W. Barber (b.1958),
> Canadian journalist, humorist, musician,
> *Bach, Beethoven and the Boys* (1986)

VOLUPTUOUS

Music arose with its voluptuous swell ...
> Lord (George Gordon) Byron (1788-1824),
> English poet,
> *Childe Harold's Pilgrimage*

VOTING

I don't think there was ever a piece of music that changed
a man's decision on how to vote.
> – Artur Schnabel (1882-1951),
> Austrian pianist, composer,
> in *My Life and Music* (1961)

WAGNER, RICHARD

Wagner's music is better than it sounds.
— Mark (Samuel Langhorne Clemens) Twain, (1835-1910),
American writer, wit.
Also attributed to Bill Nye (1850-96)

Wagner has beautiful moments but awful quarter hours.
— Gioacchino Rossini (1792-1868),
Italian composer

There is no law against composing music when one has
no ideas whatsoever. The music of Wagner, therefore, is
perfectly legal.
— review in *The National*,
Paris (Nov. 1850)

The prelude to *Tristan and Isolde* sounded as if a bomb
had fallen into a large music factory and had thrown all
the notes into confusion.
— J. Stettenheim,
review in the Berlin *Tribune* (Feb. 1873)

The Prelude to *Tristan und Isolde* reminds one of the old
Italian painting of a martyr whose intestines are slowly
unwound from his body on a reel.
— Eduard Hanslick (1825-1904),
Austrian music critic, writer
(June, 1868)

When a musician can no longer count up to three, be
becomes *dramatic*, he becomes *Wagnerian*.
— Friedrich Nietszche (1844-1900),
German philosopher, writer,
The Case of Wagner

Wagner drives the nail into your head with swinging hammer blows.
> – P.A. Fiorentino (1806-1864)

I love Wagner, but the music I prefer is that of a cat hung up by his tail outside a window and trying to stick to the panes of glass with its paws.
> – Charles Baudelaire (1821-67),
> French poet, writer

Wagner is Berlioz without the melody.
> – Daniel Auber, (1782-1871)
> French composer,
> quoted in *Le Ménestrel* (1863).

Wagner is the Puccini of music.
> – J.B. Morton (1893-1979),
> English journalist,
> who wrote a newspaper column under the name
> *Beachcomber*

We've been rehearsing for two hours — and we're still playing the same bloody tune!
> – Sir Thomas Beecham (1879-1961),
> English conductor,
> rehearsing Wagner's *Götterdammerung*

I refused to sing the young Siegfried, because I think he is a bore. I always call him a Wagnerian L'il Abner.
> – Jon Vickers (b.1926),
> Canadian operatic tenor

I like Wagner's music better than any other music. It is so loud that one can talk the whole time without people hearing what one says. That is a great advantage.
> – Oscar Wilde (1854-1900),
> Irish-English writer, wit,
> *The Picture of Dorian Gray* (1891)

Tannhäuser is not merely polyphonous, but poly-cacophonous.
>— *Musical World*, London (Oct. 1855)

After *Lohengrin*, I had a splitting headache, and all through the night I dreamed of a goose.
>— Mily Balakirev (1837-1910),
>Russian composer,
>in a letter to Vladimir Stasov (Nov. 1868)

What time is the next swan?
>— Leo Slezak (1873-1946),
>Czechoslovakian opera tenor,
>after the mechanical swan left without him
>during a performance of *Lohengrin*

It is the music of a demented eunuch.
>— *Figaro*, Paris,
>on the music of Wagner (July 1876)

Wagner, thank the fates, is no hypocrite. He says right out what he means, and he usually means something nasty.
— James Gibbons Huneker (1860-1921)
American music critic, writer

One can't judge Wagner's opera *Lohengrin* after a first hearing, and I certainly don't intend hearing it a second time.
— Gioacchino Rossini (1792-1868),
Italian composer

[Wagner's *Parsifal* is] the kind of opera that starts at six o'clock and after it has been going on for three hours, you look at your watch and it says 6:20.
— David Randolph (b.1914)

Wagner is evidently mad.
— Hector Berlioz (1803-1869),
French composer,
in a letter (Mar,1861)

Is Wagner a human being at all? Is he not rather a disease?
— Friedrich Nietzsche (1844-1900),
German philosopher, writer

WAR

After leaving New York on Sept. 11 [2001], I'm not against war. I'm against brutality. I'm not against anybody bombing anyone if they feel they have the right.
— Ashley MacIsaac (b.1974),
Canadian musician, fiddler,
quoted in the *National Post* (Apr, 2003)

Waters

Where should this music be? I' th' air, or th' earth?
It sounds no more; and sure it waits upon
Some gods o' the island. Sitting upon a bank,
Weeping agina the King my father's wrack,
This music crept by me upon the waters,
Allaying both their fury, and my passion,
With its sweet air

> — William Shakespeare (1564-1616),
> English poet, playwright,
> Ferdinand, in *The Tempest*, act 1, scene 2, line 389

There be none of Beauty's daughters
With a magic like thee;
And like music on the waters
Is thy sweet voice to me.

> Lord (George Gordon) Byron (1788-1824),
> English poet,
> *Stanzas for music* (1816)

Wedding Music

Music played at weddings always reminds me of the music played for soldiers before they go into battle.

> — Heinrich Heine (1797-1856),
> German poet, writer

WELL-TEMPERED

As a boy, I thought 'well-tempered' was a whimsical epithet for a keyboard that did not fight back at the performer.
— Anthony Burgess (1917-93),
English novelist, composer,
This Man and Music (1983)

WOMEN

Musick and women I cannot but give way to, whatever my business is.
— Samuel Pepys (1633-1703),
English diarist, writer,
Diary (March 9, 1666)

WOODWINDS

The chief objection to playing wind instruments it that it prolongs the life of the player.
— George Bernard Shaw (1856-1950),
Irish-English playwright, music critic, wit

WORDS

If a literary man puts together two words about music, one of them will be wrong.
— Aaron Copland (1900-90),
American composer

Music limps, but words give it a crutch.
>— Anthony Burgess (1917-93),
>English novelist, composer,
>*This Man and Music* (1983)

It is the little rift within the lute,
That by and by will make the music mute,
And ever widening slowly silence all.
>— Alfred Lord Tennyson (1809-92),
>English poet,
>*Idylls of the King: Merlin and Vivien*

WORDSWORTH, WILLIAM

How thankful we ought to be that Wordsworth was only a poet and not a musician. Fancy a symphony by Wordsworth! Fancy having to sit it out! And fancy what it would have been if he had written fugues!
>— Samuel Butler (1835-1902),
>English essayist, writer,
>referring to the English poet (1770-1850),
>*Notebooks* (1912)

WORK

A lot of fellows nowadays have a B.A., M.D., or Ph.D. Unfortunately, they don't have a J.O.B.
>— Fats (Antoine) Domino (b.1928)
>American singer-songwriter, piano

WORLD

Musick is the thing of the world that I love most.
— Samuel Pepys (1633-1703),
English diarist, writer,
Diary (July, 1666)

XENOPHON

The sweetest of all sounds is praise.
— Xenophon (ca.440-357B.C),
Greek soldier, writer

XERXES

In the opening aria [*Ombra mai fù* of G.F. Handel's opera *Xerxes*] ... the Persian emperor loftily serenades a beloved plane tree. He has a human beloved too, however, who most inconveniently loves his brother.
— Austin Baer,
American journalist, writer
in *Atlantic Unbound* magazine (Feb. 1997)

Xerxes: The hero of one of Handel's operas and a man with a seriously weird tree obsession. It's a *castrato* role, which may or may not have anything to do with it — depending on how much faith you put in Freud.
— David W. Barber (b.1958),
Canadian journalist, writer, musician,
in *Tenors, Tantrums and Trills* (1996)

Youth

I am perhaps the oldest musician in the world. I am an old man but in many senses a very young man. And this is what I want you to be, young, young all your life, and to say things to the world that are true.

> – Pablo Casals (1876-1973),
> Spanish cellist, writer

Zappa, Frank

Rock journalism is people who can't write interviewing people who cannot talk for people who can't read.

> – Frank Zappa (1940-93),
> American musician, composer, singer-songwriter,
> in *Loose Talk* (ed. Linda Botts, 1980)

The typical rock fan is not smart enough to know when he is being dumped on.

> – Frank Zappa (1940-93),
> American musician, composer, singer-songwriter

Zevon, Warren

There's nothing romantic, nothing grand, nothing heroic, nothing brave, nothing like that about drinking. It's a real coward's death.

> – Warren Zevon (b.1947),
> American singer-songwriter

I'll sleep when I'm dead.

> – Warren Zevon (b.1947),
> American singer-songwriter

ZITHER

The music of the zither, the flute and the lyre enervates the mind.

– Ovid (43 B.C-18 AD),
Greek poet

***

About the Editor

David W. Barber is a journalist and musician and the author of several books of humorous musical history, including *Bach, Beethoven and the Boys, If It Ain't Baroque* and *Tutus, Tights and Tiptoes,* and *The Last Laugh,* a collection of satirical essays. He's also the editor of an earlier book of musical quotes and three books in the *Quotable* series, *Quotable Alice, Quotable Sherlock* and *Quotable Twain.* Formerly entertainment editor of the Kingston, Ont., *Whig-Standard* and editor of *Broadcast Week* magazine at the Toronto *Globe and Mail,* he's now a freelance journalist and musician in Toronto. As a composer, his works include two symphonies, a jazz mass based on the music of Dave Brubeck, a *Requiem,* several short choral and chamber works and various vocal-jazz songs and arrangements. He sings with the Toronto Chamber Choir and with his vocal-jazz group, Barber & the Sevilles, which has just released their first CD, called *Cybersex.*
Visit David's Web-site at: www.bachbeethoven.com

***

BOOKS by David W. Barber & Dave Donald

A Musician's Dictionary
preface by Yehudi Menuhin
isbn 0-920151-21-3

Bach, Beethoven and the Boys
Music History as It Ought to Be Taught
preface by Anthony Burgess
isbn 0-920151-10-8

When the Fat Lady Sings
Opera History as It Ought to Be Taught
preface by Maureen Forrester
foreword by Anna Russell
isbn 0-920151-34-5

If It Ain't Baroque
More Music History as It Ought to Be Taught
isbn 0-920151-15-9

Tenors, Tantrums and Trills
An Opera Dictionary from Aida to Zzzz
isbn 0-920151-19-1

Tutus, Tights and Tiptoes
Ballet History as It Ought to Be Taught
preface by Karen Kain
isbn 0-920151-30-2

***
Better Than It Sounds
A Dictionary of Humorous Musical Quotations
isbn 0-920151-22-1
Compiled & Edited by
David W. Barber

QUOTABLE BOOKS

Quotable War Or Peace
Compiled & Edited by Geoff Savage
caricatures by Mike Rooth
preface by Bruce Surtees
isbn 0-920151-57-4

Quotable Opera
Aria ready for a Laugh?
Compiled & Edited by
Steve & Nancy Tanner
caricatures by Umberto Tàccola
isbn 0-920151-54-X

Quotable Pop
Fifty Decades of Blah Blah Blah
Compiled & Edited by
Phil Dellio & Scott Woods
caricatures by Mike Rooth
isbn 0-920151-50-7

Quotable Jazz
Compiled & Edited by
Marshall Bowden
caricatures by Mike Rooth
isbn 0-920151-55-8

Quotable Alice
Compiled & Edited by David W. Barber
illustrations by Sir John Tenniel
isbn 0-920151-52-3

Quotable Sherlock
Compiled & Edited by David W. Barber
illustrations by Sidney Paget
isbn 0-920151-53-1

Quotable Twain
Compiled & Edited by David W. Barber
isbn 0-920151-56-6

O<small>THER</small> S<small>OUND</small> A<small>ND</small> V<small>ISION</small> B<small>OOKS</small>

The Composers
A Hystery of Music
by Kevin Reeves
preface by Daniel Taylor
isbn 0-920151-29-9

1812 And All That
A Concise History of Music from
30,000 B.C. to the Millennium
by Lawrence Leonard,
cartoons by Emma Bebbington
isbn 0-920151-33-7

How to Stay Awake
During Anybody's Second Movement
by David E. Walden
cartoons by Mike Duncan
preface by Charlie Farquharson
isbn 0-920151-20-5

How To Listen To Modern Music
Without Earplugs
by David E. Walden
cartoons by Mike Duncan
foreword by Bramwell Tovey
isbn 0-920151-31-0

The Thing I've Played With the Most
Professor Anthon E. Darling Discusses
His Favourite Instrument
by David E. Walden,
cartoons by Mike Duncan
foreword by Mabel May Squinnge
isbn 0-920151-35-3

More Love Lives of the Great Composers
by Basil Howitt
isbn 0-920151-36-1

Love Lives of the Great Composers
From Gesualdo to Wagner
by Basil Howitt
isbn 0-920151-18-3

Opera Antics & Annecdotes
by Stephen Tanner
Illustrations by Umberto Tàccola
preface by David W. Barber
isbn 0-920151-32-9

I Wanna Be Sedated
Pop Music in the Seventies
by Phil Dellio & Scott Woods
caricatures by Dave Prothero
preface by Chuck Eddy
isbn 0-920151-16-7

A Working Musician's Joke Book
by Daniel G. Theaker
cartoons by Mike Freen
preface by David Barber
isbn o-920151-23-X

Selected Bibliography & Acknowlededements

Bartlett's Familiar Quotations, ed. John Bartlett; 14th
  edition ed. Emily Morison Beck (© Little, Brown, 1855, 1968)
Dictionary of Composers, ed. Charles Osborne
  (© Macmillan, 1977)
Dictionary of Musical Quotations, ed. Ian Crofton
  & Donald Fraser (© Schirmer, 1985)
Lexicon of Musical Invective, ed. Nicholas Slonimsky
  (© University of Washington, 1953-1965)
Oxford Dictionary of Modern Quotations, ed. Tony Augarde
  (© Oxford, 1991)
Quotations, ed. John Daintith (© Bloomsbury, 1987)
Shaw on Music, ed. Eric Bentley (© Doubleday, 1955)
Words About Music, ed. John Amis & Michael Rose
  (© Paragon House, 1989)
Music, A Pictorial Archive of Woodcuts & Engravings,
  by Jim Harter (© Dover Publications Inc, 1980)
Old Fashioned Music Illustrations, Carol Belanger Grafton,
  (© Dover Publications Inc, 1990)
Hector Berlioz (p.97) John Cage (p.100) Giuseppe Verdi (p.156)
Caricatures from *The Composers, A Hystery of Music*, by Kevin
Reeves (© Sound And Vision, 1998)

***

www.rollingstone.com   www.brainyquotes.com
www.vh1.com   www.vivisimo.com
www.google.com

First published in Canada by

Sound And Vision
359 Riverdale Avenue
Toronto, Canada, M4J 1A4
www.soundandvision.com
First printing, July 2003
1 2 3 4 5 6 7 8 9 10

NATIONAL LIBRARY OF CANADA CATALOGUING IN PUBLICATION DATA

The Music lover's quotation book / David W. Barber.

ISBN 0-920151-37-X

1. Music — Quotations, maxims, etc. I. Barber, David W.
(David William), 1958-
PN6084.M8B22 2003   780   C2003-903983-8

Typeset in New Century School Book
Printed and bound in Canada by Métrolitho Inc.

Note from the Publisher

My thanks to David Barber for all of his fine work over the last 20 years and for this book, which I know you will enjoy!

Sound And Vision books may be purchased for educational or promotional use or for special sales. If you have any comments on this book or any other books we publish, or if you would like a catalogue, please write or email us.

Sound And Vision,
359 Riverdale Avenue,
Toronto, Canada M4J 1A4

We are always looking for original books to publish. If you have an idea or manuscript that is in the genre of musical humour, including educational themes, please contact us. Thank you for purchasing or borrowing this book.

To view our catalogue online, please visit us at:
www.soundandvision.com

Geoff Savage
Publisher